WORLDVIEWS

A CHILDREN'S INTRODUCTION TO MISSIONS

Written by Sarah Lewis

Published by Pioneers
10123 William Carey Dr.
Orlando, FL 32832 U.S.A.

Scripture taken from New American Standard Bible (NASB).
Copyright © 1960, 1962, 1963, 1968, 1971, 1972, 1973, 1975, 1977, 1995 by The Lockman Foundation.

Scripture taken from the English Standard Version. ESV® Permanent Text Edition® (2016).
Copyright © 2001 by Crossway Bibles, a publishing ministry of Good News Publishers.

ISBN 978-0-9899545-6-3

The Team: Matt Green, Nathan Burns, Joseph Boyle, Daniel Anan, Jacob Lewis, Tim Twinem, Ben Johnson.
Illustrations by Ronald Rabideau, www.ronaldrabideau.com
Videos and Design by Parable Media, www.parable.media

Printed in the United States of America

First Edition 2017

GETTING
STARTED

This book is about your family's place in God's story of redemption. It is about how God has been moving in nations all around the world to bring people to Himself, and how you can join Him. As a family you will learn about worldviews, explore cultures, find new ways to share the Gospel, and discover God's heart for all people. As you work through this book together, here are a few symbols to be on the lookout for:

This symbol means that there is a video for you to watch. All the videos can be found on our website at world-views.com.

Whenever you see this symbol, it is a chance to stop and think things through. Talk together as a family about what you have been learning.

There will always be reasons to talk to God, especially when you are learning new things about Him. So every time this symbols pops up, make sure you take the time to pray.

SUPPLY LIST

To get the most out of your Worldviews study, you might want to consider gathering some supplies ahead of time. Here is a list of everything you will need:

TRIBAL

- pencils
- crayons or markers
- scissors
- glue
- an empty jar
- a blank picture book (or paper and a stapler to make your own)
- cornmeal
- agave
- chia seeds
- cinnamon
- material for huarache soles (rubber mats or old shoe soles work best but you can also use cardboard or craft foam)
- para cord or shoe laces
- drill and bit (optional)

HINDU

- pencils
- crayons or markers
- scissors
- glue
- Henna art kit (optional)
- whole wheat flour
- oil
- salt
- a piece of solid color fabric
- rubber stamp
- fabric paint
- sponge
- paintbrush

UNRELIGIOUS

- pencils
- crayons or markers
- scissors
- glue
- cottage cheese
- red onion
- butter
- sour cream
- paprika
- salt
- caraway seeds
- eggs
- egg dye
- red onion peel
- white crayon or wax pencil
- freshly picked leaves
- nylon stockings
- embroidery needle (or other sharp point for etching)

MUSLIM

- pencils
- crayons or markers
- scissors
- glue
- garlic
- canned chickpeas
- tahini paste
- lemon juice
- oil
- craft sand (or salt)
- food coloring
- glass jar
- funnel

BUDDHIST

- pencils
- crayons or markers
- scissors
- glue
- agar agar powder
- sugar
- coconut milk
- salt
- 12 paper clips
- 6 different colored strips of paper
- tape

THIS IS
GOD'S STORY

IN THE BEGINNING GOD CREATED THE HEAVENS AND THE EARTH. BEFORE THERE WAS LIGHT OR AIR OR WATER, GOD HAD A GREAT IDEA...

He formed our world, and He made it beautiful—full of sounds and colors and smells and tastes. He created animals and plants and stars and everything on the earth and in the sky. And then, as His last and most wonderful creation, He made people. Do you know what was so special about people? What made them different from everything else He made? God created people in His image—to be like Him and to know Him. God put a special desire in people's hearts to worship Him. And all of creation shows how worthy God is to be praised.

You may know that the story didn't end there. God had an enemy who wanted to destroy all that God had made. His name was Satan, and his goal was to ruin God's relationship with people. It didn't take long before his plan seemed to be working. The very first people God created forgot why they were created and they even started to forget how good it was to know God. They believed a lie from Satan instead of God's truth, and they turned away from God. But God already had a plan to restore His relationship with people. He promised that one day He would defeat Satan once and for all and rescue His people from all of their forgetting. They would remember why they were created, and they would remember how good it was to know and love Him.

Do you know how God would do it? It might sound like a strange plan, but God would rescue His people by sending His Son to die for them. Jesus came down from Heaven and entered earth as a person. He showed people how to worship God. And then He gave His life as a way to pay for all the mistakes people had made. He died on a cross and made a way for people to be restored to God.

This is a true story. There are many more details, but this true story is called the Gospel. Some people hear it, believe it, and follow God. Some people hear it, reject it, and follow Satan. And some people have never heard it. If you are a follower of God, then one of the most important jobs you have on earth is to share the Gospel, to tell people the story of God and the great lengths He has gone to help them know Him and love Him. That's why in this study we are going to be talking about people all over the world who don't know the story (or don't believe the story) of God. We will learn about who they are, where they live, the different things they believe, and how we can share the Gospel with them.

THINK ABOUT IT

What special place do you think God has for you in His story?

Why do you think God wants all people to hear about Him?

WHAT IS A WORLDVIEW?

A worldview is the way that a person looks at the world. It's what people believe about who they are, where they came from, and why they are here. A person's worldview is shaped by many things: where they live, what the people around them believe, what experiences they have, and what things they care most about.

If you are a follower of God and use the Bible to determine who you are, where you came from, and what you are here for, then you have a Biblical worldview. Through this study we will learn about five other major worldviews and the people who represent them.

THUMB
PRINTS

TO HELP US REMEMBER THE WORLDVIEWS
WE ARE STUDYING, WE WILL USE AN
ACRONYM CALLED THUMB.

TRIBAL

HINDU

UNRELIGIOUS

MUSLIM

BUDDHIST

Okay, so hold out your thumb. Look very closely at it. What do you notice? Can you see your fingerprint? Did you know that every person has a unique fingerprint? No two thumbs are the same. As you learn about people from all over the world, remember that they are uniquely special to God. He made every single person unique, and He wants everyone to know how special they are to Him. No matter who they are or where they come from, anyone can be a part of His story.

WRITE OUT A PRAYER TO GOD FOR THE NATIONS. ASK GOD TO GIVE YOU HIS LOVE FOR PEOPLE FROM EVERY NATION, LANGUAGE, AND WORLDVIEW.

TRIBAL

The best ways to prepare to share the gospel with someone is to learn about what they think. Let's learn about the Tribal worldview.

WATCH THE VIDEO

Learn about Tribal people by watching the Tribal video at
world-views.com/Tribal.
Fill in the blanks as you watch.

Most Tribal people believe that _____ around them have

_____ inside them. This belief system is called _____.

Almost all Tribal people have a deep sense of _____.

Some Tribal people worship their_____.

Most Tribal people do not have _____, but pass down their beliefs

through _____.

THINK ABOUT IT

What do you have in common with the tribal worldview?

What would it feel like to believe there are spirits everywhere?

Why would the gospel be important for a tribal person?

"ANIMISM"

It is hard to define exactly what Tribal people believe because there are so many different groups of Tribal people that all believe unique things. But they all have some common ideas that shape the way they view life. Almost all Tribal beliefs begin with the idea of animism. Here are some of the main things an animist believes.

HOLISM

The belief that everything that exists is connected in a spiritual way.

Because everything is connected, the animist believes that everything a person does also affects plants, animals, spirits, and all dead or living things. For an animist it is important to keep everything in balance.

SPIRITUALISM

The belief that everything is connected to the spiritual world.

There is nothing that happens on earth that is simply natural. A person getting sick is somehow a result of something happening spiritually. A person has great success in life when he or she is at harmony with the spiritual world.

POWER

The goal of life is to survive, which leads people to seek power for their benefit.

For animists, it is good to get power or knowledge any way they can to take care of themselves and their families. For them, life is a series of challenges — from growing their gardens, to avoiding sickness and death, to hunting and providing food. They find power through the spirit world using sacred dances and ceremonies as a way to manipulate and appease spirits to help them.

COMMUNITY

It is important to belong to and work for the community around you.

Animists believe that they are connected in a special way to the people and things around them. They look to their community to define what is right and wrong, and to decide how to think about life. Community is important for protection, health, happiness, and power. Keeping harmony within the community is very important. An animist may even see lying and manipulating as a great way to keep the harmony.

PRAY ABOUT IT

Spend some time today praying for Tribal people. Pray that through Jesus they would be freed from the fear and oppression of spirits, ancestors, and war.

TELLING
THEM

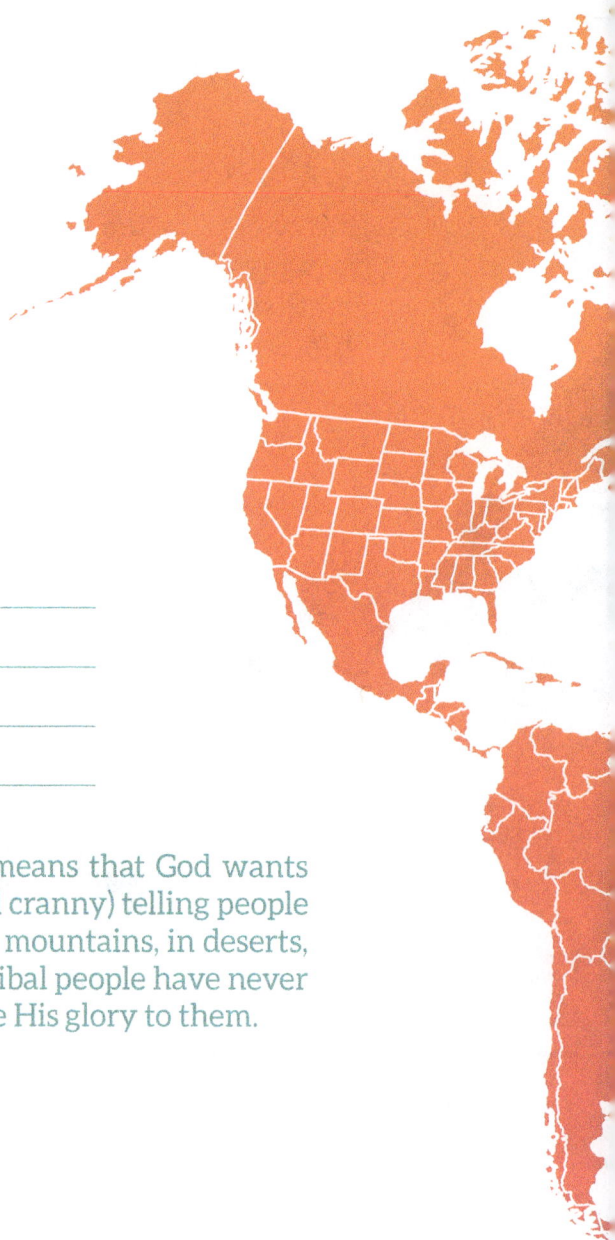

LOOK UP PSALM 96:3 AND WRITE IT ON THE LINES BELOW:

_____

_____

_____

_____

God wants the whole world to hear about His love. That means that God wants people to go to the very ends of the earth (in every nook and cranny) telling people about Him. Tribal people live deep in jungles, high up in the mountains, in deserts, and even on islands. Because they are hard to visit, many Tribal people have never heard about Jesus. God is looking for people who will declare His glory to them.

? THINK ABOUT IT

What would it be like to live in a remote place?

Far from the grocery store, or the doctor's office, or the mall?

Where would you like to go to tell Tribal people about God's love for them?

TRIBA

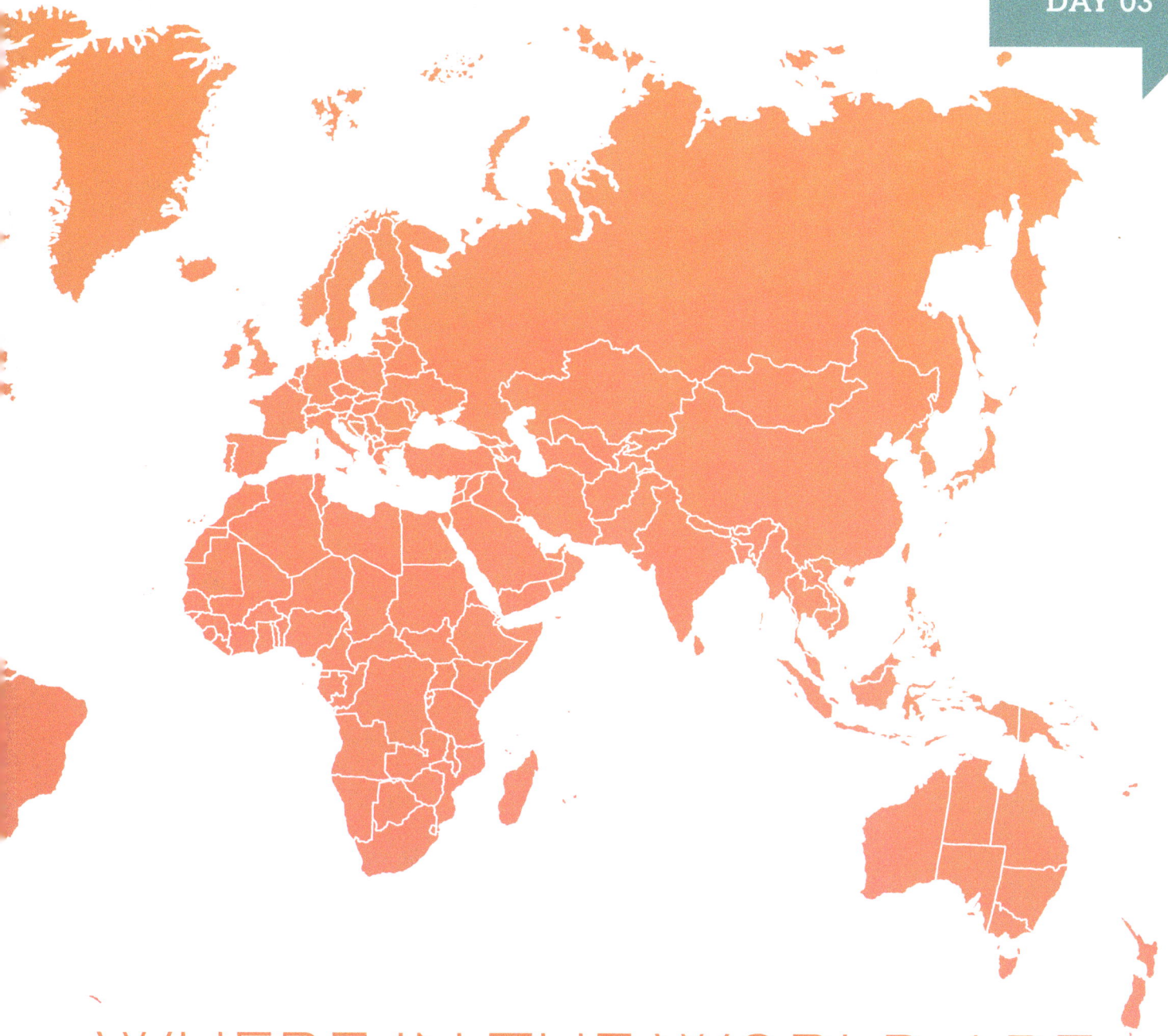

WHERE IN THE WORLD ARE
L PEOPLE?

CIRCLE THESE COUNTRIES ON THE MAP WHERE TRIBAL PEOPLE CAN BE FOUND:

Mexico Ethiopia Nigeria Brazil Papua New Guinea Peru Colombia

  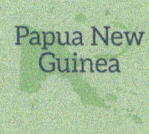

DO CHRISTIANS AND TRIBAL PEOPLE HAVE THE SAME

WORLDVIEW?

What does the Bible say about the way a Tribal person views the world? Read through some Tribal beliefs and then look up the corresponding Bible verses to see how they match up. After reading the verse, write down what the Bible says and how that Tribal belief compares.

ORIGINS

Most Tribal people believe the world was created. There are many different stories of how it was formed, but most Tribal groups think a very powerful spirit created the world.

JEREMIAH 10:12
_____
_____
_____
_____

COLOSSIANS 1:16
_____
_____
_____
_____

GOD

Most Tribal people believe in one spirit that is more powerful than the rest. Some believe that the spirit is a part of nature like an animal or the sun, while others believe that the spirit always existed and is very different from anything in nature.

PSALM 90:2
_____
_____
_____

Some Tribal groups believe this spirit sees and hears everything that happens on earth but isn't involved in any of it. Most Tribal groups do not believe this spirit has any personal interest in them. They do not feel loved or known by the spirit.

PSALM 139:7-10
_____
_____
_____
_____

Tribal people believe that there are spirits who can interact with things in the world. Spirits can live inside of objects in nature. These spirits aren't as powerful as the creator spirit but are still feared. Some Tribal people believe in good and bad spirits that fight against each other, while other Tribal groups think of spirits as just angry or pleased depending on your actions.

JOSHUA 24:14
_____
_____
_____
_____

EPHESIANS 6:11-17
_____
_____
_____
_____

MAN

Most Tribal people see humans as an important part of creation. People were made to live in harmony with the spirits inside plants and animals and to take care of the earth.

GENESIS 1:26-27

_____
_____
_____
_____

Most Tribal people don't think much about the future. They worry about what is happening at the moment and how to make themselves and their families safe, happy, and healthy every day.

MATTHEW 6:25-34

_____
_____
_____
_____
_____

Tribal people believe that spirits can be bribed and manipulated. They believe it is important to learn how to control spirits so that the spirits will do what they want them to do. Gaining power is one of the most important goals of a Tribal person's life.

DEUTERONOMY 10:17

_____
_____
_____
_____

Tribal people believe that there is only a limited amount of good in the world. You shouldn't want good things to happen to other people because it means that it won't happen for you. They feel threatened by anyone else's happiness.

2 CORINTHIANS 9:8

_____
_____
_____

SIN

Most Tribal groups do not believe that the creator spirit has any interest in a relationship with them. They do not think of sin as something that separates them from God because they already view themselves as separate. To them, sin is something that separates them from the community, family, or friends. Sin is not a concept they deal with as we understand sin. To an animist it is a sense of "right and wrong" or "good or bad." For example, if I steal, then the community doesn't like it. Stealing breaks trust with the community and the person wronged, so I shouldn't do it. For a Tribal person, sin is a social thing, not a spiritual problem.

PSALM 51:4

_____
_____
_____
_____

Most Tribal people believe that bad things happen because of the spirit world or because of sorcery from another person. Nothing happens by accident or natural causes. Sickness and death, lack of food or rain, or failure in hunting are caused by spirits that are angry or by someone who has placed magic on them. If they feel the spirits are angry, then they will do certain rituals that appease the spirits to make them happy again.

ROMANS 6:23

_____
_____
_____
_____

Tribal people don't believe that God is the standard for right and wrong. They decide what is right based on what is beneficial. If you can do something to make yourself happier, it is the best thing to do.

ROMANS 14:12

_____
_____
_____
_____

SALVATION

Because they don't see sin as spiritual, Tribal people don't see the need for salvation from God. They feel that their sin needs to be forgiven by the people or by the spirits around them.

ACTS 4:12

_____
_____
_____
_____

Tribal people believe that they can make their sin right by performing special ceremonies or making sacrifices to the spirits. Doing these things in the proper way will help clear them of any wrong doing.

HEBREWS 9:28

_____
_____
_____
_____

? THINK ABOUT IT

Some Tribal beliefs are similar to what the Bible says. How could God use that to help you connect with a Tribal person?
Some Tribal beliefs are very different from what the Bible says. How could you use that as an opportunity to share the gospel with them?

DEATH

Tribal people believe that death is the result of evil spirits harming or cursing that person. Death does not happen as a part of God's plan but as a result of bad actions.

PSALM 139:15-16

_____
_____
_____
_____

Most Tribal people believe that when a person dies, a part of him or her lives on as a spirit. That spirit might return to earth and live inside of a different part of nature (like a tree or an animal) or that spirit might join ancestors in a special place.

ECCLESIASTES 12:7

_____
_____
_____

Most Tribal groups fear the spirits of dead people because they believe that the spirits can still do good things or bad things to them. Tribal people often pray to the spirits of dead people, trying to convince them to offer help or strength.

JOB 14:10-12

_____
_____
_____
_____

SHARING
GOD'S STORY

How would you tell a Tribal person about Jesus?

Many Tribal groups live in remote places still today. In a Tribal culture, it isn't always important to have a written language, so some Tribal groups don't read or write. They learn by hearing and memorizing, and they are really good at it! Many times, important information is learned by storytelling to make it more interesting and easier to remember.

So if you wanted to share the gospel with a Tribal person, you probably wouldn't want to simply hand them a Bible. You'd want to tell them a story. Can you think of a story from the Bible that would communicate important information to a Tribal person? Think about what Tribal people struggle with, what they fear, what they love, what they hate; then think of a story from the Bible that would be special to them.

After you've decided on a story, memorize the main parts and turn it into a picture book. Tell your story to a friend or parent. Practice how you would say it...who knows, maybe someday you can use your picture book to bring God's message to a Tribal person!

WRITE DOWN WHICH STORY YOU CHOSE AND WHY YOU THINK IT WOULD BE IMPORTANT TO A TRIBAL PERSON

PRAY ABOUT IT

Pray that Tribal people would hear stories about God's power and believe that He can save them.

TRIBAL
BIBLE VERSE

Write John 10:10 on the lines below. Most Tribal people live in a system where their lives are constantly threatened. The enemy of God wants to destroy any hope they have of a future. He wants to see them live in fear and loss and devastation. But God wants Tribal people to know that He came to rescue them from the forces of darkness that surround them. He came to bring life and hope. Have you thought of God's heart for Tribal people? As you color this verse, use it as a way to remember the fears that Tribal people face and the freedom that God desires for them. Ask God how He might want to use you to bring them His message of hope.

_____

_____

_____

_____

_____

_____

_____

THINK ABOUT IT

What does it mean to have an abundant life?

Who is the thief that comes to steal, kill, and destroy?

How does he work to oppress Tribal people?

Why would this verse be good news for a Tribal person?

THE THIEF COMES ONLY TO STEAL AND KILL AND DESTROY. I CAME THAT THEY MAY HAVE LIFE AND HAVE IT ABUNDANTLY.

- JOHN 10:10

THE CULTURE

Now that you have learned so much about the Tribal worldview, let's learn about a group of Tribal people. They are called the Tarahumara people, and they live in the mountains of Mexico.

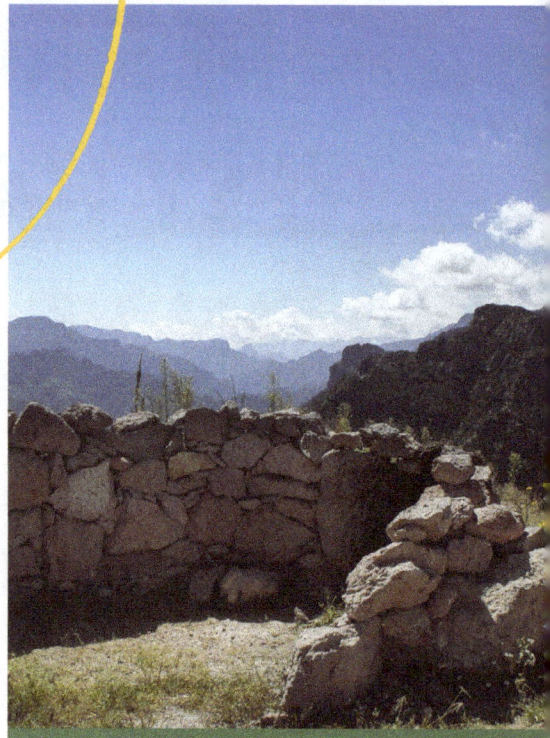

Tarahumara people live in the deserts of Mexico. It is rough terrain with very high plateaus and very low ravines. There are deep gorges carved out by winding rivers, which are the Tarahumara's main source of water.

Their homes are made of adobe, which is a mud mixture. These adobe walls are very efficient for insulation. Most families have tin roofs provided by the government. However, in the most remote places they still use wood beams cut from trees, with mud for insulation.

The desert canyons where the Tarahumara people live are dry most of the year. Without much rainfall, plants have to be hardy to survive. If you're ever visiting Copper Canyon, watch out for cacti.

The Tarahumara people are very good at weaving. They weave bowls and plates out of grass. They also make nice wool blankets to keep themselves warm during the cold winter.

Tarahumara women love to wear brightly colored dresses and long flowing skirts. When they wear their traditional clothing, they stand out and look very beautiful against the desert landscape.

RUN LIKE THE
TARAHUMARA

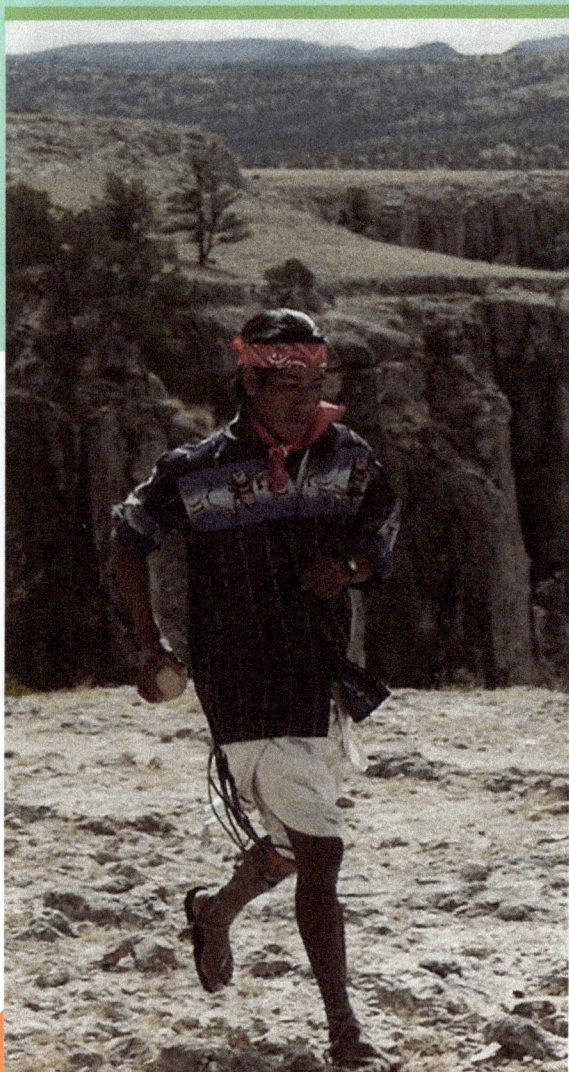

The Tarahumara people are known for their ability to run. Because their houses are often separated by deep gorges, it can take up to several days to walk to a neighbor's house. To cut down on travel time, Tarahumara people learned to run long distances with great endurance.

They can run for such long distances that they hunt animals by chasing them (sometimes for days). After being chased for so long, the animal gets too tired to run anymore and lies down.

The Tarahumara also have a favorite game called rarajípari. In this game, teams run chasing after a ball for up to 100 miles to see who can get their ball across the finish line first.

Most of the time the Tarahumara people run wearing special sandals they make from old tires. They call these sandals huaraches. Traditional huaraches have thin rubber soles cut in the shape of the foot. The rubber is tied onto the feet using heavy string or leather straps.

WANT TO GIVE IT A TRY?
Follow the steps on the next page to make your own pair of huaraches.

YOU'LL NEED:
- 1 pair of scissors
- material for the soles (cardboard, craft foam, rubber mats, old shoe soles)
- 2 cords or laces (about 5" long each)
- Drill and bit (optional)

PRAY ABOUT IT

As you create your huaraches, take some time to pray for Tribal people. Pray that they would hear about the God who created them and loves them.

1

Trace the outline of your normal shoe onto your shoe material. Trace your left shoe on one sheet and your right shoe on another; then cut them out.

2

Put your feet on the cutouts and mark a dot between your big toe and the toe next to it. Repeat for the other foot.

3

Make a mark on the sole halfway between your toes and your heel on the left side of your foot. Do the same for the right side of your foot. Repeat for the other foot.

4

Using the scissors (or drill bit), poke small holes through the marks on the sole.

5

Tie a knot (bigger than the hole you made) on the end of your cord. Thread the cord through the top hole so that the knot is under the sole.

6

Thread the cord through the outside hole from top to bottom. Then loop it around itself from the front toward the back. Repeat for inside hole.

7

Slip your foot in and tie the cord by bringing it around the ankle and then up through the cord that lies on top of your foot.

8

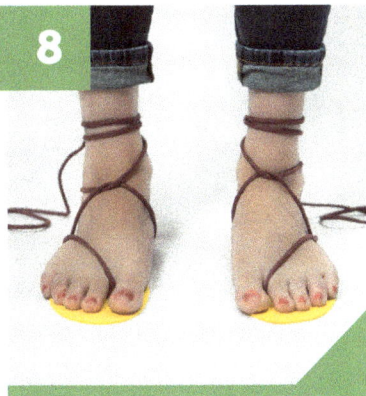

Wrap the cord around your leg once or twice depending on the leftover length.

9

Tie any excess string where it feels comfortable.

EVERYONE NEEDS TO EAT

Why not try something new?

Consider making these Kobisi energy bars like the ones the Tarahumara people eat. You could even invite a friend over to share your bars with. Be sure to tell them all that you have been learning about the Tarahumara people and God's heart for Tribal people everywhere.

PRAY ABOUT IT

Thank God for all that you have learned and ask Him what He might want you to do with the new things you know.

THINK ABOUT IT

What is the most exciting thing you have learned?

Have you learned anything that has changed the way you think?

Kobisi Energy Bars

ingredients

1 cup cornmeal
2/3 cup water
3 tablespoons agave
2 tablespoons chia seeds
a dash of cinnamon

directions

Step One:
Preheat the oven to 350ºF.

Step Two:
Toast the cornmeal in a pan on medium heat until it becomes slightly brown (about 5 minutes).

Step Three:
Add all the ingredients to a food processor and pulse until there are no large chunks remaining. If the mixture is too crumbly, add a little more water until you're left with a thick paste.

Step Four:
Form the mixture into small bars. Bake on a nonstick tray for about 10-12 minutes until the outside forms a solid crust and begins to show small cracks. Remove from the oven, let cool, and enjoy!

EAT LIKE THE
TARAHUMARA

Many of the foods that the Tarahumara people eat are made from the plants and vegetables they can grow on their land. One important food for the Tarahumara is called Kobisi. Kobisi is made out of corn and different spices. It can be used to make many different things including a kind of oatmeal paste and energy bars. Sometimes it is simply added to a glass of water and used as a source of energy on a long journey. Making Kobisi can be hard work, but it is a valuable staple for the Tarahumara people.

First, corn kernels are taken off the cob. Then the corn is roasted over a fire until it is browned (sometimes it even pops into popcorn). After it has cooled, the roasted corn is ground for a long time between two stones until it turns into a powdery consistency. Spices are added to help flavor the powder, and the Kobisi is ready to be used.

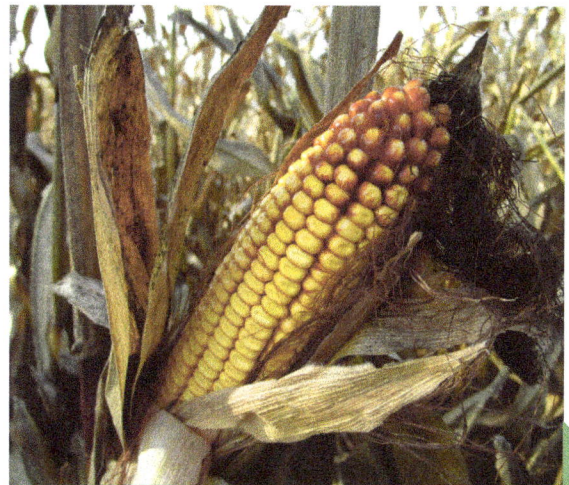

WANT TO GIVE IT A TRY? FOLLOW THE RECIPE ABOVE TO SEE IF YOU ENJOY EATING LIKE THE TARAHUMARA.

HINDU

The second worldview we will look at is the *Hindu* worldview. Let's learn about what Hindus believe.

WATCH THE VIDEO

Learn about Hindu people by watching the Hindu video at world-views.com/Hindu Fill in the blanks as you watch.

Hinduism has over _____ million gods. Each of these gods is considered a part of the supreme god _____.

To be united with Brahman, you must live many different _____. The belief that after a person dies, he or she comes back to live a different life on earth is called _____.

Hindus believe that the choices you make will result in either a better life or a worse life. This idea is known as _____.

Hindus believe that each person has a responsibility to live a _____ life. When they do, it creates _____ in the universe. This is called _____.

THINK ABOUT IT

Do you think it's important to make good choices? Why or why not?

What do you think happens to a person when they make bad choices?

DHARMA

"BOTH-AND"

Hinduism can be a tricky thing for most non-Hindu people to understand. It is complex, and different Hindus might emphasize different Hindu beliefs. Hindu people also feel that it is perfectly natural for contradictions to occur within their beliefs because people were made to discover truth for themselves. This makes the Hindu worldview complicated and hard to define. Here are a few examples:

GOD

Hindus believe in a creator god that is both existence and nonexistence. They believe that he is active and inactive. Different from people, but also people are a part of him. They believe that god is one god, but also many gods.

VEDAS

The Hindu worldview is built on the Vedas: their sacred scriptures. They believe that the Vedas are ultimate authority, but that everyone can interpret them differently. The four Vedas are all equally important and authoritative, but it is not required to know or study all of them. Each person can decide which Vedas he or she wants to emphasize in life.

TRUTH

Hindus believe that there is one truth, but that truth is different for everyone. They believe that there is a path to Brahman but that everyone can find his or her own path.

WORSHIP

Rituals are an important part of a Hindu's life. They perform many rituals to worship and honor the gods. But, ritual acts of worship are also thought to be ignorant and do not lead to spiritual liberation.

PRAY ABOUT IT

Spend some time today praying for Hindu people. Pray that they would discover the one true way to salvation through Jesus.

DISCIPLE
MAKER

LOOK UP MATTHEW 28:19-20 AND WRITE IT ON THE LINES BELOW:

_____

_____

_____

_____

When Jesus left earth, He gave His followers a very important job. Every follower of Jesus is a disciple maker. It's our special duty to go into every nation around the world telling people the good news of Jesus and teaching them how to follow Him. Hindu people can be found in many nations but most of them live in India and the countries around it. God is looking for people who will go to them.

THINK ABOUT IT

What does it mean to be a disciple maker?

What would it be like to baptize a Hindu person who has decided to follow Jesus?

HIND

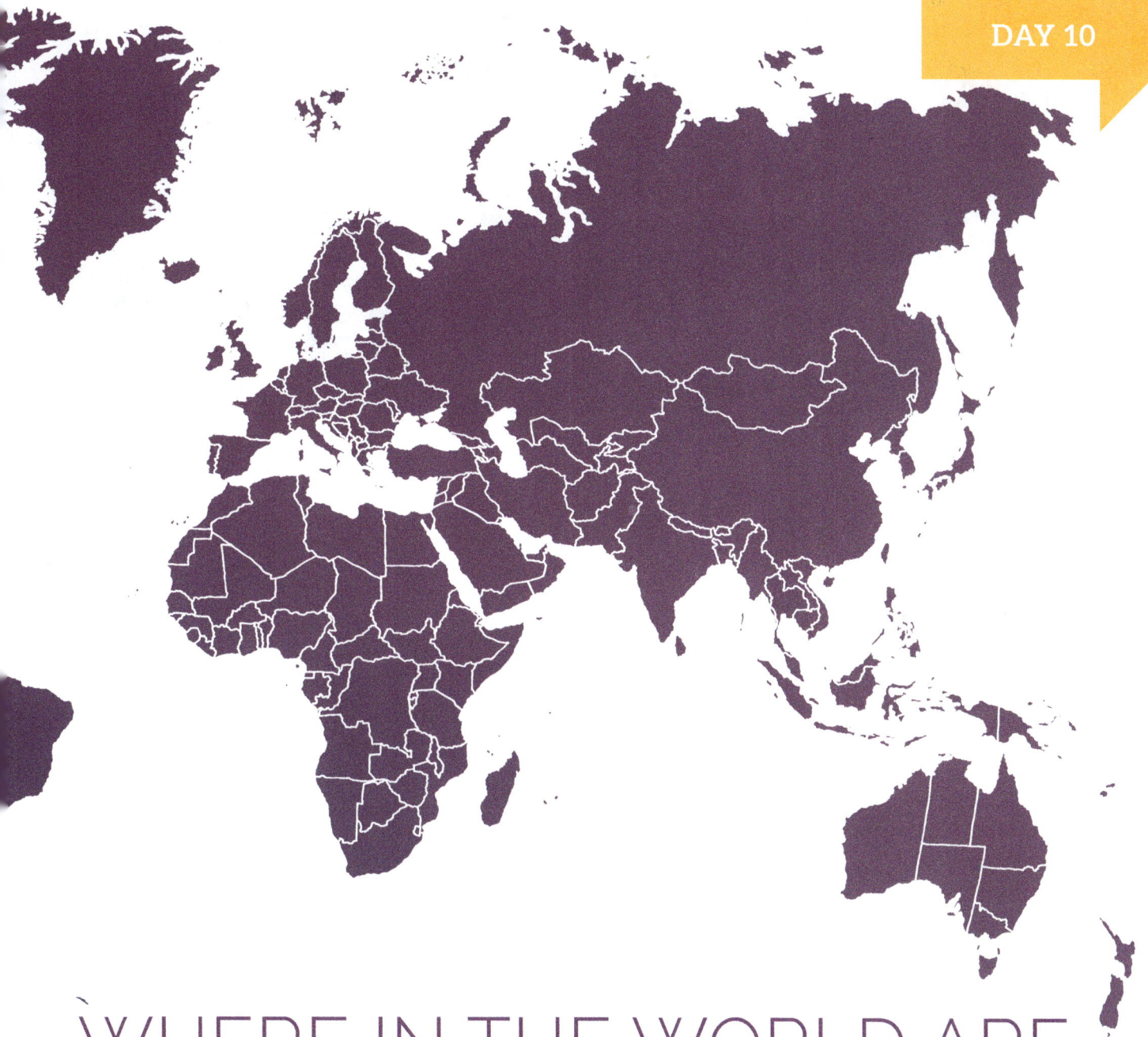

WHERE IN THE WORLD ARE
U PEOPLE?

CIRCLE THESE COUNTRIES ON THE MAP WHERE HINDU PEOPLE CAN BE FOUND:

 India   Nepal   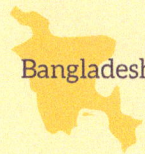 Sri Lanka   Bangladesh   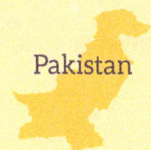 Bhutan   Pakistan

DO CHRISTIANS AND HINDU PEOPLE HAVE THE SAME
WORLDVIEW?

What does the Bible say about the way a Hindu person views the world? Read through some Hindu beliefs and then look up the corresponding Bible verses to see how they match up. After reading the verse, write down what the Bible says and how that Hindu belief compares.

ORIGINS

Hinduism says that the world was created by Brahma, the son of the supreme god Brahman.

JOHN 1:1-4 _____
_____
_____
_____
_____

Hindus believe that the universe exists for only one of Brahma's days. One day for Brahma is equal to 4 billion years for humans. That means that a Hindu believes that every 4 billion years the whole universe dissolves away and is recreated again.

ISAIAH 66:22 _____
_____
_____
_____

ECCLESIASTES 1:4 _____
_____
_____
_____
_____

GOD

Hindu people believe in a god that is one god, but also many gods. Brahman has many parts that are known and understood through many different gods.

1 TIMOTHY 2:5 _____
_____
_____
_____
_____

In Hinduism everything is considered a part of Brahman. The universe and everything in it is one with Brahman. There is only one thing god cannot do: separate himself from people.

ISAIAH 55:8-9 _____
_____
_____
_____
_____

Hindus believe that no religion is the only right way to God. You can be united with God through many different understandings of who He is and through many different religions.

JOHN 14:6 _____
_____
_____
_____
_____

MAN

Hindus believe that deep down everyone is perfect and that life is about discovering and living up to that perfection. They believe that man shares the same qualities and duties as God.

MARK 7:21-23 _____
_____
_____
_____
_____

Hindus believe in karma. They believe that you can control your own destiny by the way you think and act. If you do good things, you will gain good things in this life and in the next. If you do bad things, you will suffer bad things in this life and in the next.

EPHESIANS 2:8-9 _____
_____
_____
_____
_____

GALATIANS 6:8-9 _____
_____
_____
_____
_____

Hinduism says that it is a person's job to maintain balance in the universe by making good choices. People have the ability to keep the universe working properly or to throw it off balance.

COLOSSIANS 1:17 _____
_____
_____
_____
_____

HEBREWS 1:3 _____
_____
_____
_____
_____

SIN

Hindu people do not see sin as something that can make a person lose salvation. If a person sins, he or she will pay for it through the law of karma.

MATTHEW 25:31-46 _____
_____
_____
_____
_____

Hindus believe that the consequence for sin is sorrow and suffering in this life, and reincarnation again on the earth.

ROMANS 6:23 _____
_____
_____
_____
_____

2 CORINTHIANS 7:10 _____
_____
_____
_____
_____

In Hinduism, god does not eternally punish evil-doers. He does not stand in judgment but allows all people infinite chances to get things right.

ECCLESIASTES 12:14 _____
_____
_____
_____
_____

2 CORINTHIANS 5:10 _____
_____
_____
_____
_____

SALVATION

Hindus believe that there are seven stages that they need to walk through to try to earn forgiveness of sins on earth: admission, remorse, repentance, confession, showing shame, penance, and reconciliation.

1 JOHN 1:9 _____
_____
_____
_____
_____

Hinduism has a concept of salvation called moksha. Moksha means "release." Hindus believe that we do not need to be saved from sins but from our own existence. To achieve moksha means that a Hindu will gain eternal bliss as they enter union with Brahman.

JOHN 17:3 _____
_____
_____
_____
_____

To achieve moksha a Hindu can choose between several different paths. One is the "way of works." This path is about perfectly following the Vedas to purify your soul. The second is the "way of knowledge." On this path people try to meditate and focus their thoughts to gain understanding of how to become one with god. The third is the "way of devotion." This path is about choosing one Hindu god to worship. If your worship is good enough, that god will help you enter moksha.

EPHESIANS 2:8 _____
_____
_____
_____
_____

DEATH

Hindu people believe in life after death. They believe that people have souls that are eternal.

JOHN 3:16 _____
_____
_____
_____
_____

Hinduism says that the soul is reincarnated on earth in another human body or even an animal. The soul is reborn many times and lives many lives on earth in the journey toward Brahman.

JOB 14:10-12 _____
_____
_____
_____
_____
_____

THINK ABOUT IT

Some Hindu beliefs are similar to what the Bible says. How could God use that to help you connect with a Hindu person?

Some Hindu beliefs are different from what the Bible says. How could you use those differences to share the Gospel?

SHARING
GOD'S STORY

How would you tell a Hindu about Jesus?

In India, one of the ways that women display beauty is through an art form called henna. Women draw beautiful symbols on a part of their body (usually their hands or feet). These images represent different things and form patterns that tell stories. Did you know that you can use henna to tell a Hindu woman about Jesus? Let's use the story of the Prodigal Son. As you read through the story, think of the main ideas. How would you represent these ideas through symbols or patterns? Use the template below to draw your designs.

Read Luke 15:11-32. Why would this story be important for a Hindu? Think through the main points of the story and how to illustrate them. Don't make your designs too complicated. You can use simple symbols to represent important ideas. If you happen to meet a Hindu in your own culture, consider telling him or her the story of the Prodigal Son and the forgiveness that God offers. Better yet, invite the person over and tell the story as you do henna together.

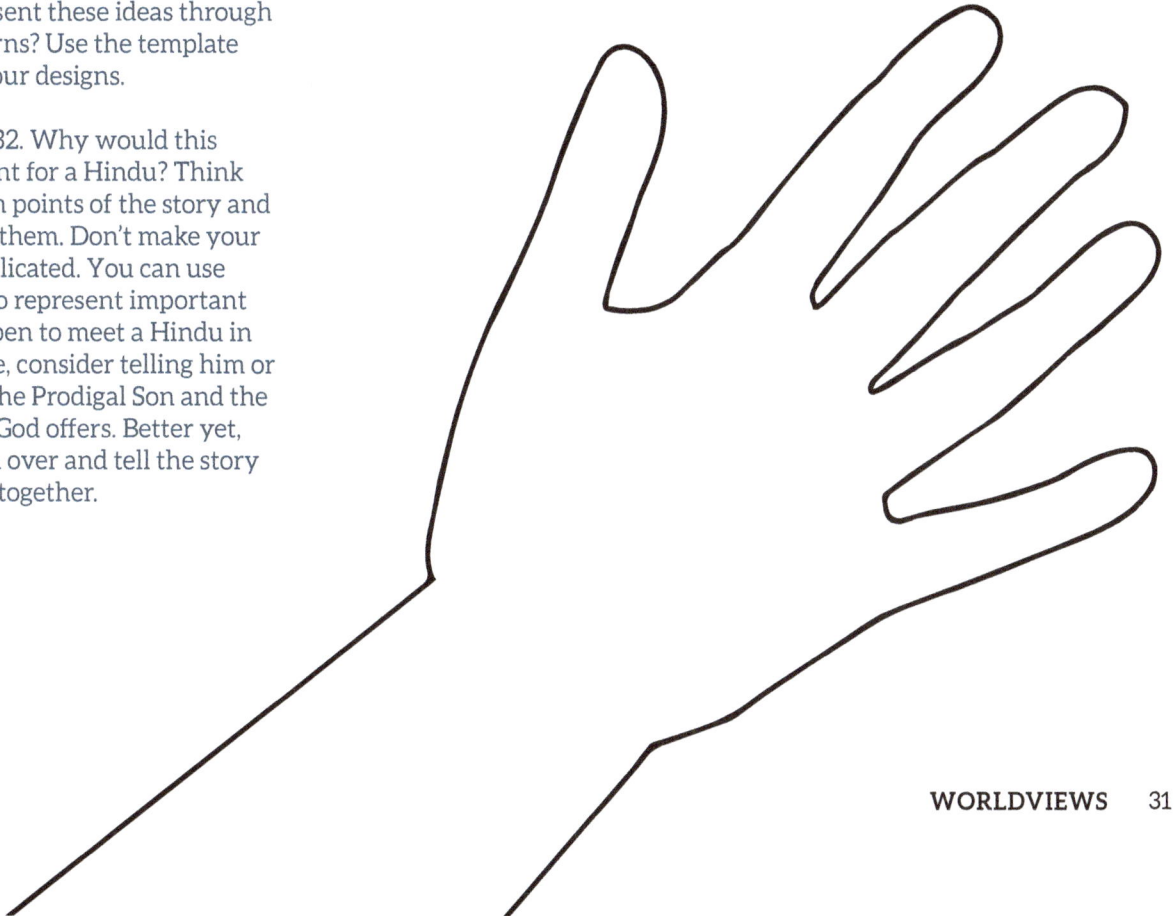

HINDU
BIBLE VERSE

Write Matthew 11:28 on the lines below. In Hinduism there is a seemingly endless cycle of birth, death, and rebirth. They believe a person lives many lives on earth trying hard to reach moksha (unity with Brahman). Although they try to avoid it, it is hard for people not to become entangled in worldly things. It is tiring and discouraging to think that they will face reincarnation again and again until they finally learn to overcome their own weaknesses.

Jesus has a different message for Hindus. They can't overcome sin on their own, but Jesus offers hope. He has done the work so that people can rest in Him and what He has already accomplished. God wants Hindus to know the peace that is found in assurance of forgiveness. Use this verse to remember the weariness that Hindus face and the rest that God desires for them. Ask God how He might want to use you to bring His message of hope to Hindu.

_____

_____

_____

_____

_____

_____

THINK ABOUT IT

What does the word weary mean?

Why do Hindu people experience weariness?

What makes you feel weary?

Where do you find rest from weariness?

come to me,
all who are
weary and
heavy-laden,
and i will give
you rest.

-matthew 11:28

THE
CULTURE

A person's worldview can be influenced by the culture he or she lives in. Read about how people live in India and imagine what it would be like to grow up in their culture.

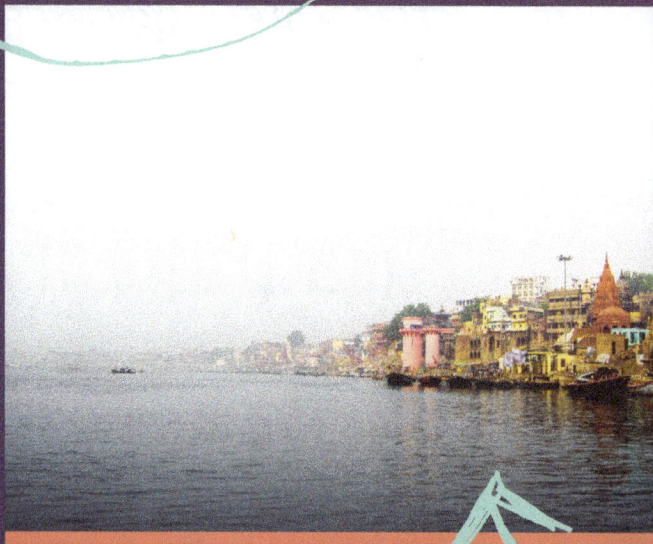

India is a country with over a billion people living in it. Every crowded street is full of colors, noises, and smells. Some people live in rural areas, but most people live in the large cities. Because it is crowded, most people ride in little vehicles called rickshaws to get around.

India is known for its beautiful architecture. Many buildings are colorful and have very elaborate carvings and decorations. One of the most famous buildings in India is called the Taj Mahal.

Traditionally, women wore beautiful dresses called saris. Saris are made from one long piece of fabric that is wrapped around the waist and then draped over one shoulder.

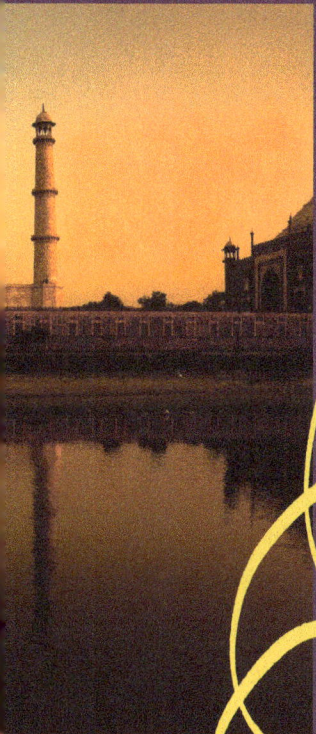

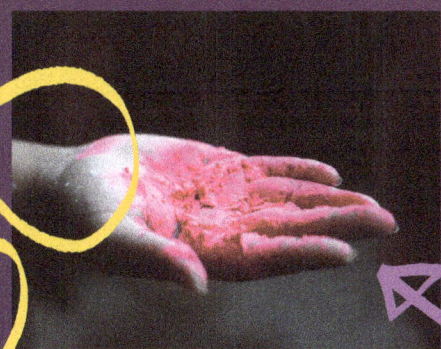

You won't have to walk far in India to run across one of their many idols. Because they have millions of gods, they are depicted everywhere. They are often painted with bright colors and presented with food offerings.

If you are ever in India around springtime, you might find yourself drenched in colorful powder from head to toe. During the Holi festival everyone throws vibrantly dyed powder at friends and family members to celebrate the coming season.

CRAFT LIKE THE
PEOPLE OF INDIA

India is full of many bright and beautiful fabrics. For hundreds of years India has produced high quality cotton, silk, and wool textiles. These textiles are used to make everything from traditional clothing to purses, pillows, and even shoes.

The cotton fabrics are made from cotton plants grown on the farms in rural India. Silk is made from wild silk moths that live in the northeastern part of the country. Wool is made from the fleece of goats that live in the mountains.

Many Indian families support themselves by making things out of these fabrics. They sew things like purses and stuffed animals that are sold all over the world.

WANT TO GIVE IT A TRY?
Follow the instructions to make your own Indian fabric.

YOU'LL NEED:
- solid fabric
- fabric paint
- paint brush
- dry sponge
- rubber stamps

PRAY ABOUT IT

As you create your own fabric, take some time to pray for the people of India. Pray that they would hear about the God who created them and loves them.

1

Find a flat surface and spread your fabric out.

2

Brush your paint onto the dry sponge.

3

Carefully dip your stamp into the paint and then place it onto your fabric.

4

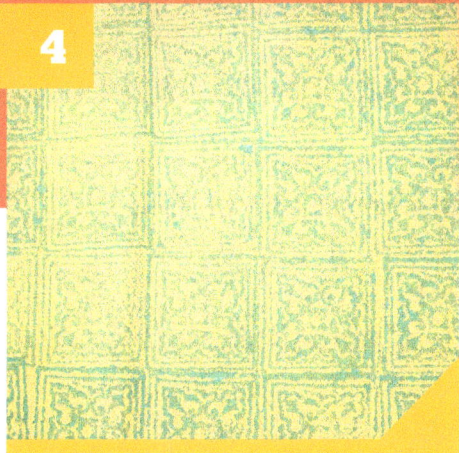

Continue until you have completed your design or pattern.

5

Allow your fabric to dry for 24 hours. And your fabric is complete!

EVERYONE NEEDS TO EAT

Why not try something new?

Consider making this paratha bread like people do in India. If you want to be really authentic, you'll also need some spicy curry to dip it into. Think about inviting a friend over to share your paratha bread with. Be sure to tell them all that you have been learning about the people of India and God's heart for Hindu people everywhere.

PRAY ABOUT IT

Thank God for all that you have learned and ask Him what He might want you to do with the new things you know.

THINK ABOUT IT

What is the most exciting thing you have learned?

Have you learned anything that has changed the way you think?

Paratha

ingredients	directions
2 cups whole wheat flour	**Step One:** In a bowl mix the flour, salt, oil, and a splash of water. Knead into a ball of dough, adding more water as needed. Cover and set aside for 30 minutes.
1-2 teaspoons oil	**Step Two:** Pinch a medium sized ball from the dough and dust with flour. Flatten to about 4 inch diameter with a rolling pin.
1/2 teaspoon salt	
water	**Step Three:** Spread a bit of oil on the surface of the dough and then fold in half. Repeat once more.
splash of oil (for roasting)	
	Step Four: Dust again with flour and use the rolling pin to flatten to a circle about 7 inches in diameter.
	Step Five: Sauté in a skillet over medium heat until lightly golden on each side. Serve warm.

EAT LIKE THE
PEOPLE OF INDIA

Indian food is probably best known for its many potent spices. They use a variety of seasonings such as chili pepper, black mustard, coriander, cardamom, turmeric, ginger, and cumin. Many of these spices are also very colorful and can even be used as dye. So if you ever go to India, expect a lot of color and a lot of flavor!

In almost every Indian home there is a version of a flatbread called paratha. Paratha is a simple unleavened bread used to dip into curry made from all those potent spices. There are many variations, but they all begin with a basic flour recipe.

WANT TO GIVE IT A TRY? FOLLOW THE RECIPE ABOVE TO SEE IF YOU ENJOY EATING LIKE THE PEOPLE OF INDIA.

UNRELIGIOUS

The third worldview we will look at is the *Unreligious* worldview. Let's see what Unreligious people believe.

WATCH THE VIDEO

Learn about Unreligious people by watching the Unreligious video at world-views.com/Unreligious. As you watch, fill in the blanks below.

Most Unreligious people believe that scientific discoveries prove that the earth has no _____.

The idea that nothing spiritual or supernatural happens is called _____.

An Unreligious person believes that there is no _____ aspect to humanity and that people stop _____ after they die.

Believing in the human ability to solve problems and make right decisions without God's help is called _____.

THINK ABOUT IT

What do you think science tells us about a Creator?

What would it be like to believe that life on earth is all there is?

What things do you believe in that you have never seen before?

"WITHOUT GOD"

Unreligious people come from many walks of life and have rejected religion for many different reasons. Some come from religious backgrounds, and others have no experience with religion at all. Because there are so many different ways to be Unreligious, we will talk through some of the main Unreligious groups below:

ATHEISTS

Atheists are people who do not believe that a god of any kind exists. Most Atheists don't describe themselves as "anti-God" or "against God," because they don't believe that there is a God to be against. They are better described as "without God" or "godless."

AGNOSTICS

Agnosticism says that God may or may not exist but that it is impossible to know. Agnostics believe that we shouldn't try to understand what can't be understood. Some believe that we may find out more about the existence of God in the future, while others believe we will never know anything about God.

FREE THINKERS

Free-thinking people decide what to believe based on logic and evidence. They think that what can't be proven shouldn't be believed. They also think that if what someone believes doesn't make logical sense, it should be rejected.

HUMANISTS

Humanism is based on the belief that everyone should be free to give life meaning for themselves. Humanists believe that they can understand life through their own ability to think, observe, and define the world around them. Humanists believe that people are able to solve problems and live fulfilling lives without God.

PRAY ABOUT IT

Spend some time today praying for Unreligious people. Pray that they would experience the reality of God's love in their lives.

BEING
LIGHT

LOOK UP ACTS 13:47 AND WRITE IT ON THE LINES BELOW:

_____

_____

_____

_____

Have you ever thought of yourself as a light? Well God says that's exactly what His followers are! He wants us to be like a bright beacon in the midst of darkness. Why? Because He wants His salvation to reach to the very ends of the earth! Unreligious people live all over the world (probably even in your neighborhood). Maybe God wants you to be a light to them.

THINK ABOUT IT

What does it mean to be a light?

How would being a light bring salvation?

Who were the Gentiles and how are they similar to Unreligious people?

UNRELIG

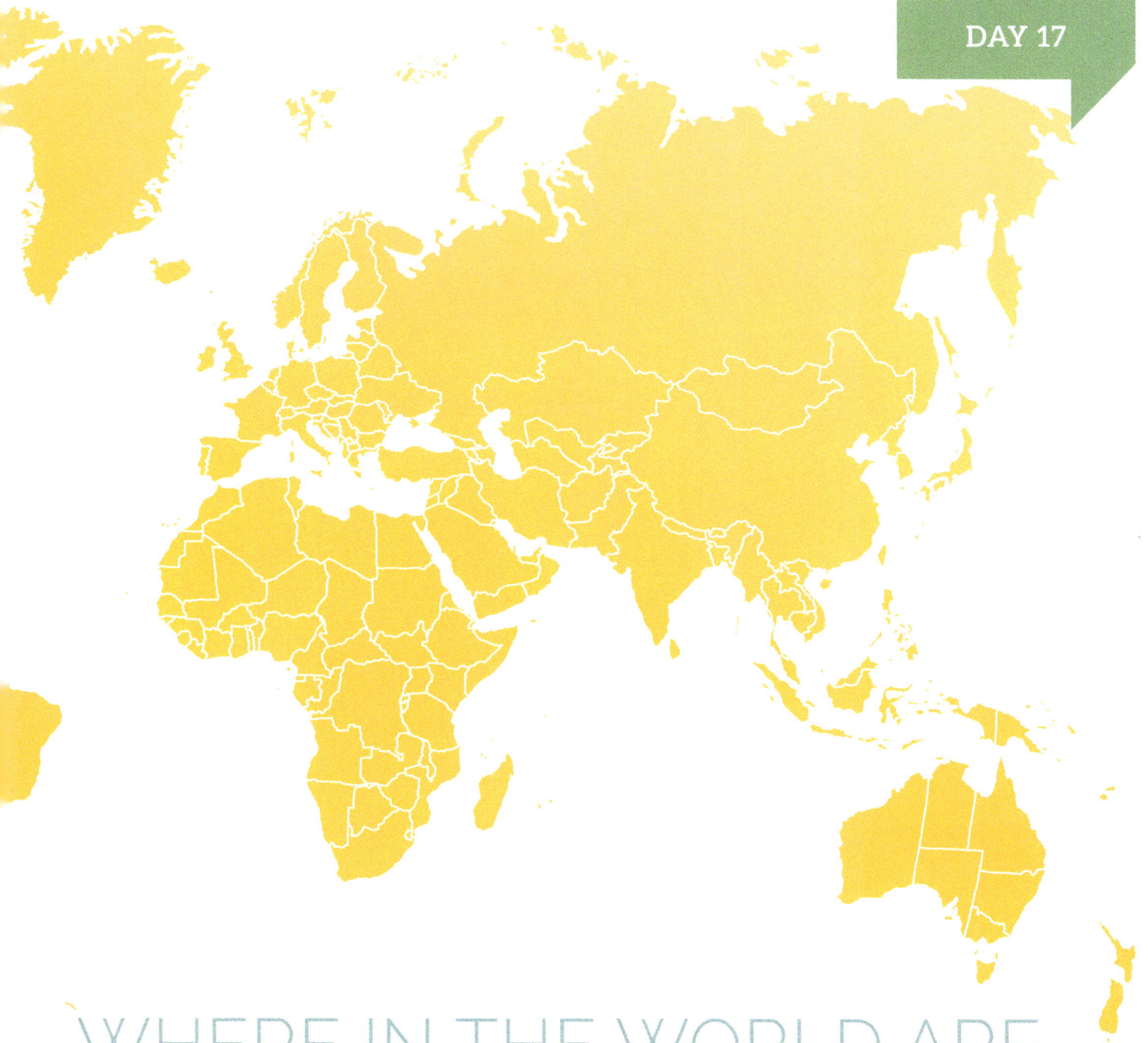

WHERE IN THE WORLD ARE
IOUS PEOPLE?

CIRCLE THESE COUNTRIES ON THE MAP WHERE UNRELIGIOUS PEOPLE CAN BE FOUND:

Ireland   Germany   France   Italy   Finland   Hungary   China

DO CHRISTIANS AND UNRELIGIOUS PEOPLE HAVE THE SAME
WORLDVIEW?

What does the Bible say about the way an Unreligious person views the world? Read through some Unreligious beliefs and then look up the corresponding Bible verses to see how they match up. After reading the verse write down what the Bible says and how that Unreligious belief compares.

ORIGINS

Most Unreligious people believe that the universe has either always existed or is the product of nature, having no creator and without design.

GENESIS 1:1-25

Some Unreligious people believe that the earth may have been created by God but then God left it alone and people have been without Him.

PSALM 139:1-12

GOD

Most Unreligious people do not believe in a God. They believe God is an idea invented by people.

PSALM 10:4

ROMANS 1:20

Some Unreligious people believe that there might be a god of some sort but that he is so unknowable that it is not important to try to understand him.

EPHESIANS 3:14-19

Some Unreligious people believe that there is a god but that he has no interest in people and so people should take no interest in him.

PROVERBS 8:17

2 CHRONICLES 7:14

MAN

Most Unreligious people do not believe that man has any significant reason for existing, but that we are simply a product of nature. Man is simply an animal that has evolved further than other animals.

GENESIS 1:26-28

_____
_____
_____
_____

Many Unreligious people believe that man's most important goal is happiness and self-fulfillment. All human effort should be directed at achieving those goals.

GALATIANS 6:8

_____
_____
_____
_____

Most Unreligious people believe that man is the ultimate authority. They are the best judge of what is right for themselves and what will bring the most fulfillment. They do not need to look to God, but only to themselves.

JEREMIAH 9:23-24

_____
_____
_____
_____

PROVERBS 14:12

_____
_____
_____
_____

SIN

Unreligious people believe in right and wrong, but do not believe that God is the one who decides what is right or wrong.

ROMANS 3:20

_____
_____
_____
_____

PROVERBS 16:1-2

_____
_____
_____
_____

For most Unreligious people, sin is social and cultural and not spiritual. Sin is not disobedience to God. Sin is doing something that is harmful to another person or to culture as a whole.

JAMES 4:4

_____
_____
_____
_____

Many Unreligious people use happiness as a gauge to decide if something is harmful to a person. They ask themselves, "Do my actions help that person be happy or do my actions make them sad?" Many choices are based on a desire to make themselves or others around them happy.

MATTHEW 5:2-12

_____
_____
_____
_____

HEBREWS 12:11

_____
_____
_____
_____

SALVATION

The concept of salvation comes from needing to be saved from judgment. Because Unreligious people usually don't believe in a god who is judge, they do not believe there is a need to be saved from his judgment.

ROMANS 2:12-16
_____
_____
_____
_____
_____

Some Unreligious people believe that if there is a god, he will offer salvation to everyone so it isn't important for anyone to base their lives on making sure they receive salvation.

MARK 16:16
_____
_____
_____
_____

THINK ABOUT IT

Some Unreligious people care about the same things Christians care about. How could God use that to help you connect with an Unreligious person?

Most Unreligious beliefs differ from what the Bible says. How could you use those differences to share the Gospel?

DEATH

Most Unreligious people do not believe that there is any form of life after death. Because people are a part of nature, they stop existing when their bodies stop working.

ACTS 24:15
_____
_____
_____
_____

JOHN 11:25
_____
_____
_____
_____

Because most Unreligious people don't believe in life after death, they see death as a motivation to gain all you can from life here and now.

ROMANS 8:18
_____
_____
_____
_____
_____

MATTHEW 6:19-21
_____
_____
_____
_____

SHARING
GOD'S STORY

How would you tell an Unreligious person about Jesus?

In many Unreligious cultures truth is seen as less important than action. In other words, people tend to care more about what kind of person you are than what you think is true. In an Unreligious culture people might ask questions like "Why is that person so kind?" or "What makes that person such a hard worker?" These questions provide the opportunity to talk about Jesus. A great way to share the Gospel with an Unreligious person is to show the Gospel to an Unreligious person.

Friendship is the key. Through your friendship, Unreligious people will be able to watch your life and start to see that you are different. It might take many months before they begin to ask you questions, but if you are a good friend, they will want to know why. Think of some ways that you could show the Gospel through friendship. What would it look like in school? in sports? in your neighborhood? Think of some questions they might ask as they watch your life. How would you answer those questions? In America it is very likely that you will have Unreligious friends. Put some of your ideas into practice and pray that as you show them the Gospel, God will give you the chance to share the Gospel as well.

For each scenario think of one way that you could display the Gospel, what question your action might make someone ask, and what answer you could give to point them to Jesus.

YOU ARE MISSING YOUR FAVORITE HAT AND YOU FIND OUT A FRIEND OF YOURS STOLE IT FROM YOU...

ACTION: _____

_____

QUESTION: _____

_____

RESPONSE: _____

_____

A NEW FAMILY MOVES IN ACROSS THE STREET...

ACTION: _____

_____

QUESTION: _____

_____

RESPONSE: _____

_____

A NEIGHBOR'S LAWN IS FULL OF LEAVES AND THEY ARE OUT OF TOWN...

ACTION: _____

_____

QUESTION: _____

_____

RESPONSE: _____

_____

PRAY ABOUT IT
Pray that Christians would become great friends to Unreligious people and share the good news with them.

UNRELIGIOUS
BIBLE VERSE

Write 1 Corinthians 2:9 on the lines below. Many Unreligious people are swayed by what they can see and explain. They don't understand God's ways, and they can't believe in something that seems too good to be true. For some Unreligious people, this leaves an emptiness in their hearts. God created us to need hope, salvation, and satisfaction that this world can't offer. He put longings inside our hearts and needs deep within ourselves that only He can meet. And He did that to point people to Himself. He has something in store for those who love Him that is so unbelievable, it can't even be imagined in our wildest dreams.

God wants Unreligious people to know Him and love Him. He wants them to experience His goodness and to have a hope that is more substantial than anything in this world. As you memorize this verse, think about people who try to find all of their hope and meaning in this world, and pray that they would be given eyes that look to what is unseen rather than to what is seen.

_____

_____

_____

_____

_____

_____

_____

THINK ABOUT IT

What is God preparing for those who love Him?

Why would that be good news for Unreligious people?

Why would this be hard for an Unreligious person to believe?

BUT
JUST AS
IT IS WRITTEN,
"THINGS WHICH
EYE HAS NOT SEEN
AND EAR HAS NOT HEARD,
AND WHICH HAVE NOT
ENTERED THE HEART OF
MAN, ALL THAT GOD HAS
PREPARED FOR THOSE
WHO LOVE HIM."

-1 CORINTHIANS 2:9

THE CULTURE

Now that we have learned so much about the Unreligious worldview, let's learn about a group of Unreligious people called Hungarians.

Traditional Hungarian homes are made out of clay and have thatched roofs. The clay is compressed into very thick walls that help keep the home warm in the winter and cool in the summer.

Hungary is a country in Europe that has beautiful rolling hills and grassy fields, as well as bustling cities. If you venture into the countryside, you might even spot a castle or two.

Hungarians have many forms of art but they are best known for their embroidery. They use colorful thread and make beautiful decorations on fabrics of all kinds.

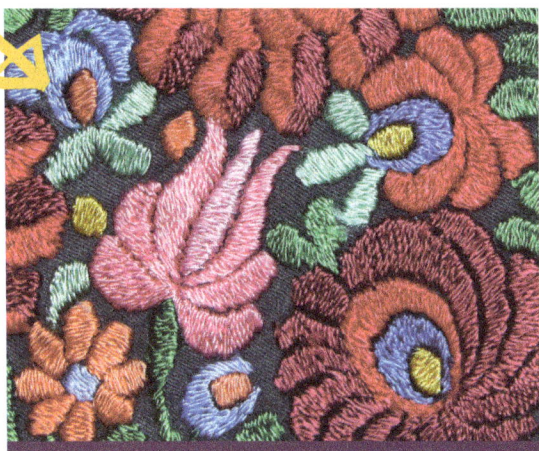

Traditional Hungarian clothing is very vibrant and detailed. Women wear dresses with carefully embroidered patterns that are often stitched by hand.

It might seem strange to see so many churches in an Unreligious culture, but Hungary wasn't always Unreligious. Christianity was officially welcomed into the country around AD 1000.

CRAFT LIKE
HUGARIANS

Hungary has many different forms of folk art, but there is nothing quite like the way they decorate eggs. Most of the time these eggs are dyed using different colorful foods boiled in water. The peel of a red onion works particularly well.

There are several methods that are used to create designs. One method is to use a hot wax pen called "íróka." Another method is to secure small leaves tightly against the eggs before dying them, leaving the pattern of the leaf on the egg. Still other methods include etching patterns into dyed eggs, or painting beautiful designs.

Decorating eggs is a tradition that began in Hungary as a way to celebrate Easter. Many of the patterns used on eggs were symbols that told the story of Jesus' death, burial, and resurrection.

WANT TO GIVE IT A TRY?
First boil red onion skin in hot water until the water has been dyed red. Next choose a method to decorate your eggs. Or give them each a try and decide which one you like the best!

YOU'LL NEED:
- all methods: hard-boiled eggs
- all methods: red onion peel
- all methods: large pot of water
- wax method: white crayons
- batik method: freshly picked leaves
- batik method: nylon stockings
- etching method: embroidery needle

PRAY ABOUT IT
As you create your eggs, take some time to pray for Hungarians. Pray that they would hear about the God who created them and loves them.

ETCHING METHOD

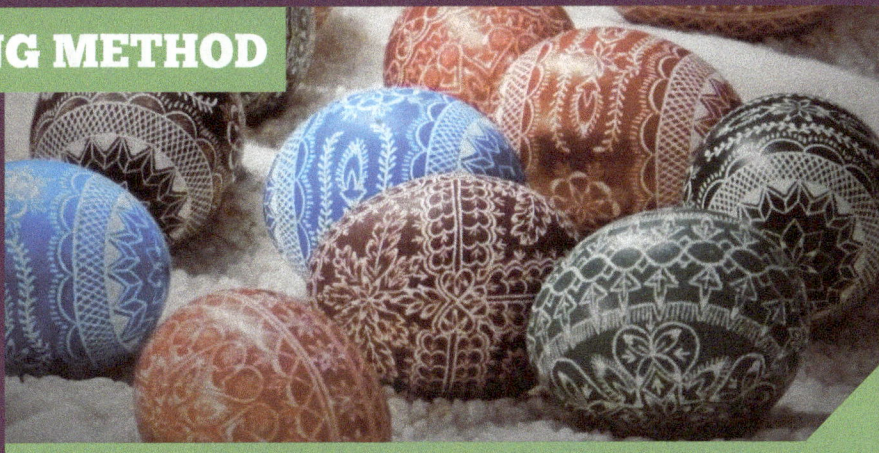

Allow eggs to soak in dye until they reach desired depth of color. Then take them out and dry the shells. Using an embroidery needle (or another sharp object) etch your designs into the egg. You will see your artwork is etched in white and contrasts the dyed parts of the shell.

BATIK METHOD

Dip a freshly picked leaf in water to get it slightly wet. Place the leaf against the shell so it sticks to the egg. Wrap the egg tightly in nylon and tie the ends to keep everything in place. Allow eggs to soak in dye until they reach desired depth of color. Once the leaf is removed, its imprint will be left on the egg.

WAX METHOD

Using a white crayon, draw designs on the egg-shell. Soak in dye until eggs reach desired depth of color. Run your dyed eggs under hot water to melt away the wax. Your design should remain white while the rest of the egg is dyed.

EVERYONE NEEDS TO EAT

Why not try something new?

You might not be able to say the word **Körözött** but you can still whip up some of this delicious cheese spread. Invite a friend over to share your meal with. Talk to them about the children of Hungary and all that you have learned about the Unreligious worldview.

PRAY ABOUT IT

Thank God for all that you have learned and ask Him what He might want you to do with the new things you know.

THINK ABOUT IT

What is the most exciting thing you have learned?

Have you learned anything that has changed the way you think?

Körözött

ingredients	directions
1 cup cottage cheese	**Step One:**
1 finely chopped red onion	In a small bowl blend cottage cheese with butter and sour cream.
1/3 cup butter	**Step Two:**
1 heaping tablespoon sour cream	Mix in all other ingredients.
1 teaspoon ground paprika	**Step Three:**
1/2 teaspoon salt	Chill in fridge for 2-3 hours.
1/2 teaspoon ground caraway seeds	**Step Four:**
	Serve with fresh bread.

EAT LIKE THE
HUNGARIANS

Many of the foods that people eat in Hungary are based on farming. Many meats and seasonal vegetables are used to create various stews, soups, and goulash. They also use a lot of milk in their cooking and are known for their unique cheeses. Much of their cheese is produced by sheep farms.

One of the most abundant flavors you will find in Hungary is paprika. It is a bright red spice that is used in almost everything they make. One appetizer combines their love of cheese and their love of paprika into a creamy dip called körözött.

WANT TO GIVE IT A TRY? FOLLOW THE RECIPE ABOVE TO SEE IF YOU ENJOY EATING LIKE THE HUNGARIANS.

MUSLIM

The fourth worldview we will look at is the *Muslim* worldview.
Let's learn about god's heart for Muslim people.

WATCH THE VIDEO

Learn about what Muslim people believe by watching the
Muslim video at world-views.com/Muslim As you watch, fill
in the blanks below

Muslim people follow the religion of _____, which means _____.
They believe in a holy book called the _____, and in a prophet named
_____.

Muslim people do many things to _____ favor with Allah like praying _____
times a day, and fasting during their holy month of _____.
They believe that one day everyone will be brought back to life and
receive _____ based on their _____. Those who have done
_____ to please Allah will enter _____ with him.

THINK ABOUT IT

What kinds of things do you do to
please God?

Do you believe these things earn
you anything? Why or why not?

QUR'AN

"FIVE PILLARS"

Islam has many different parts and some varying beliefs but there are five main things Muslims have to do in order to be truly Muslim. They are called the Five Pillars of Islam:

TESTIMONY OF FAITH

There are special words that must be spoken. A person has to say and believe that Allah is the only god (without a partner or a son), and that Muhammad is his messenger. This is the first thing a person must do to become Muslim.

FASTING

Every year Muslims celebrate a holy month called Ramadan. During Ramadan Muslims do not eat or drink anything from sunrise to sunset every day. This is considered a way to spiritually purify yourself.

PRAYER

A Muslim must perform specific prayers in specific ways. Prayers are performed at dawn, noon, afternoon, sunset, and night. As they pray, they must face the direction of the city of Mecca and say special words.

GIVING ZAKAT

Muslims believe that they can purify their possessions by giving a certain portion of what they have to those in need. They are required to give specific amounts of specific possessions to specific people.

HAJJ

All Muslims must do their best to make one journey to Mecca during their lifetime. This journey is called Hajj. If you are healthy enough and have enough money, then you must go to Mecca as a special way to devote yourself to Allah.

PRAY ABOUT IT

Spend some time today praying for Muslim people. Pray that they would believe in Jesus as God's Son and begin to follow Him.

BEING A
WITNESS

LOOK UP ACTS 1:8 AND WRITE IT ON THE LINES BELOW:

_____

_____

_____

_____

Jesus left us with a big job. It's so big that He knew we would need His help. He gives us power through His Spirit so that we can be witnesses for Him throughout the whole world. Did you know that many Muslim people live very close to where Jesus lived on earth? In fact, there are Muslim people in Jerusalem, Judea, and Samaria who are still waiting to meet a powerful witness of Jesus.

THINK ABOUT IT

What would it be like to walk where Jesus walked?

What does it mean to be a witness?

Where would you like to go to witness to a Muslim person?

MUSL

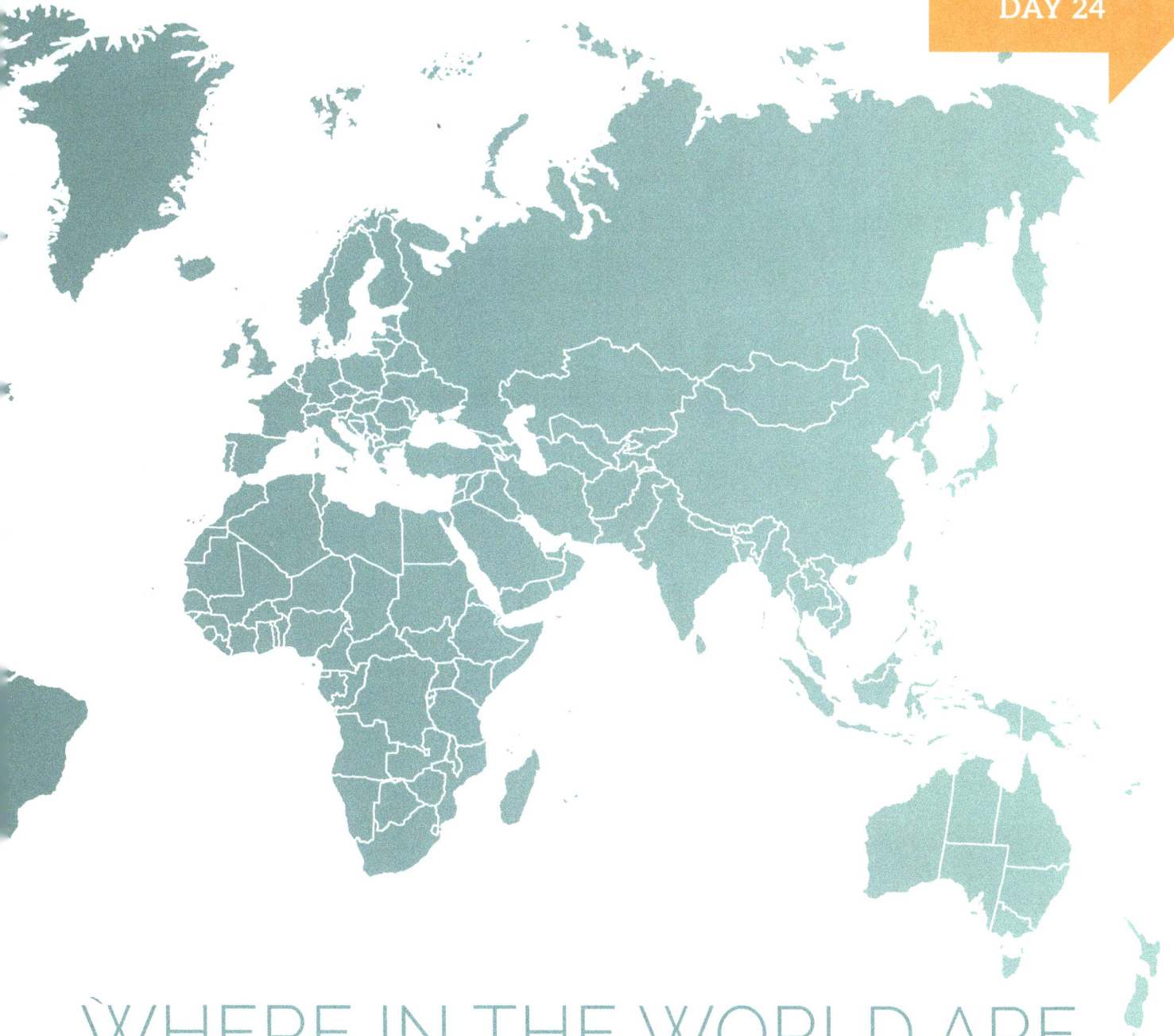

WHERE IN THE WORLD ARE
M PEOPLE?

CIRCLE THESE COUNTRIES ON THE MAP WHERE MUSLIM PEOPLE CAN BE FOUND:

Iraq　　　　Syria　　　　Indonesia　　　　Chad　　　　Turkey　　　　Afghanistan

DO CHRISTIANS AND MUSLIM PEOPLE HAVE THE SAME

WORLDVIEW?

What does the Bible say about the way a Muslim person views the world? Read through some Muslim beliefs and then look up the corresponding Bible verses to see how they match up. After reading the verse write down what the Bible says and how that Muslim belief compares.

ORIGINS

Muslims believe that Allah created the world and everything in it. The Qur'an says that Allah made the earth in six spans of time.

GENESIS 1:1-31 _____
_____
_____
_____
_____

GOD

Muslim people believe that there is one god and he has always existed. He is the maker of all things and the sustainer of all things. He is called the first, the last, and the eternal god.

REVELATION 22:13 _____
_____
_____
_____
_____

PSALM 90:2 _____
_____
_____
_____

For a Muslim, one of the most important things to believe about Allah is that he is not a trinity, and has no persons, or partners.

MATTHEW 28:19 _____
_____
_____
_____

COLOSSIANS 1:15-20 _____
_____
_____
_____
_____

Muslims believe that Allah created everything totally different from himself. Nothing in all creation resembles him in any way.

GENESIS 1:26 _____
_____
_____
_____

ROMANS 1:20 _____
_____
_____
_____

MAN

Muslims believe that people were made by Allah as a unique and special part of his creation. People have a soul, a conscience, knowledge, and free will.

PSALM 139:13-14 _____
_____
_____
_____
_____

Muslims believe that life is a test and that the purpose of man's life on earth is to pass the test by obeying Allah.

2 TIMOTHY 1:9 _____
_____
_____
_____
_____

EPHESIANS 2:10 _____
_____
_____
_____
_____

In Islam, there are many important rules to obey to keep yourself pure before Allah. Muslims must wash their bodies in certain ways, avoid certain foods, keep certain rituals, and pray in certain ways.

COLOSSIANS 2:20-23 _____
_____
_____
_____
_____

SIN

In Islam, bad thoughts are not sin if a person decides not to act on them. It isn't what you think or how you feel that is sinful, but only disobedient actions that need forgiveness.

2 CORINTHIANS 10:5 _____
_____
_____
_____
_____

PHILIPPIANS 4:8 _____
_____
_____
_____
_____

For a Muslim, not all sin is the same. If you do something only slightly bad, you can cover it up by performing the right prayers or ritual washing. But if you do something really bad, you must repent and hope that Allah will forgive you.

EPHESIANS 2:1-3 _____
_____
_____
_____
_____

JAMES 2:10 _____
_____
_____
_____
_____

SALVATION

In Islam, people are born pure and without sin. Everyone is born with their salvation intact. It is your duty on earth to do all that you can to maintain that status.

PSALM 58:3
_____
_____
_____
_____
_____

ROMANS 5:12
_____
_____
_____
_____
_____

According to Islam, a person can be saved by their works. Allah is merciful and will forgive us for our failures if we do the very best we can to worship him well. A person will not know if their works have saved them until judgment day.

TITUS 3:4-7
_____
_____
_____
_____
_____

ROMANS 3:20
_____
_____
_____
_____
_____

DEATH

Muslims believe that when people die, their souls stay in the grave until Allah raises them from the dead. The soul and body experience either torment or pleasure depending on the person's actions during their life.

PSALM 103:12
_____
_____
_____
_____
_____

Muslims believe that on judgment day everyone will be brought back to life and held accountable for their actions. If they did enough to please Allah, they will be in paradise. If they didn't do enough to please Allah, they will be in punishment. Both places are eternal.

1 CORINTHIANS 15:51-58
_____
_____
_____
_____
_____

THINK ABOUT IT

Some Muslim beliefs are similar to what the Bible teaches. How could God use that to help you connect with a Muslim person?

Many Muslim beliefs are very different from what the Bible says. How could you use those differences to share the Gospel?

SHARING
GOD'S STORY

How would you tell a Muslim person about Jesus?

A very important part of the Muslim culture is to be hospitable. Friendship and trust are built in homes as people invite one another in for tea or for a meal. Many Muslim families living in America have never been invited into an American home. They wonder what it looks like, how we act at the dinner table, where we keep our shoes.

If you have the opportunity to meet Muslims here in America, invite them over for tea and get to know them. Ask them about their lives and how they got here. When they ask you about your life, be ready to talk about Jesus and why you follow Him. Think about five main ways God has worked in your life that might have special significance for a Muslim. Be sure to include those aspects of God in your personal story. Practice sharing your story with a friend or family member over a cup of tea.

Write down your personal life story. Sometimes it helps to narrow it down to five big things that have happened in your life and how God was a part of those things.

1 _____

2 _____

3 _____

4 _____

5 _____

PRAY ABOUT IT

Pray that believers would share with Muslims what God has done in their lives. Pray that Muslims would believe in Him through their stories.

MUSLIM
BIBLE VERSE

Write down Romans 8:38-39 on the lines below. For Muslims there is no guarantee that they will be in paradise with Allah. They hope that they have done enough to please him, but they do not believe that it is possible to know for sure if they will be saved. This leaves many Muslims feeling unsettled and uncertain of their eternal destiny.

God offers a sure hope to those who believe in His Son. If you have been saved through Jesus, then nothing can separate you from God's love. You don't have to wait and see where you're going because Jesus is already preparing a place for you in Heaven. Muslims need to know about the sure hope that is found in Jesus. Use this verse to help you remember how God wants Muslim people to experience His unbreakable love.

_____

_____

_____

_____

_____

_____

THINK ABOUT IT

What does it mean to have assurance of salvation?

How does someone receive God's unbreakable love?

What would it be like to live without assurance of salvation?

for i am
sure that neither
death nor life, nor angels no
rulers, nor things present nor
things to come, nor powers, nor height
nor depth, nor anything else in all creation,
will be able to separate us from the love of
god in christ jesus our lord.

-romans 8:38-39

THE
CULTURE

Now that you have learned so much about the Muslim worldview, let's learn about some Muslim people. They are the Syrian people of the Middle East.

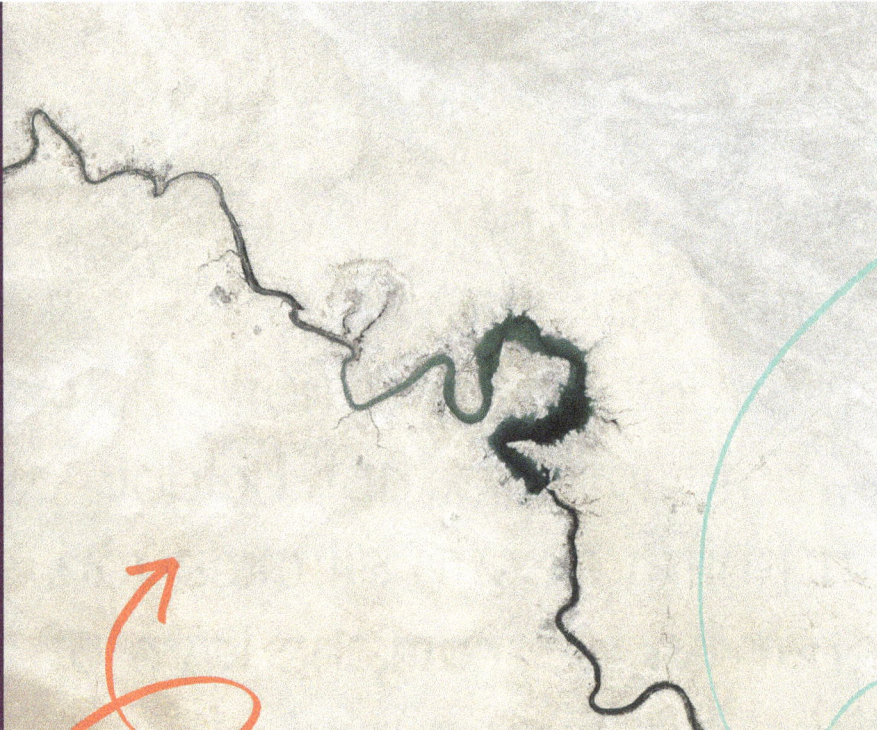

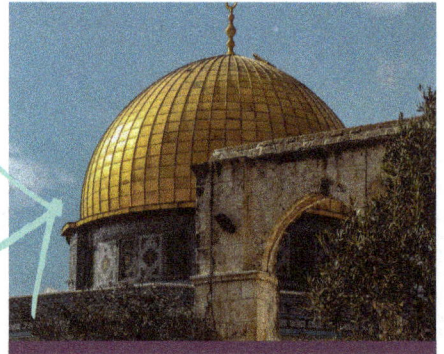

The Middle East is a large region that covers many countries. It's mostly vast desert with sloping sand dunes and dusty winds. It's pretty hot, so if you're ever in the area, make sure you have plenty of sunscreen and water!

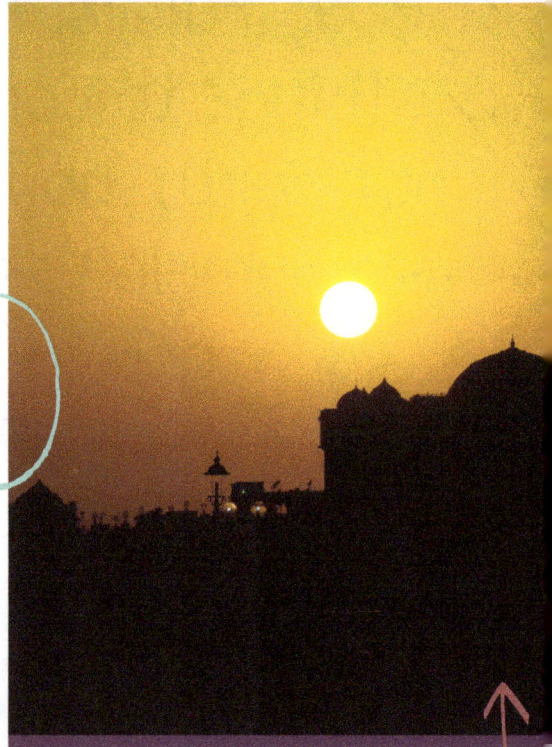

Mosques are buildings the Muslims gather in to pray and worship Allah. They are built in many different ways but usually can be recognized by their domes and arches.

Sometimes traveling across the desert can be dangerous. For hundreds of years people have relied on camels to carry them safely through the dry lands. They are called ships of the desert.

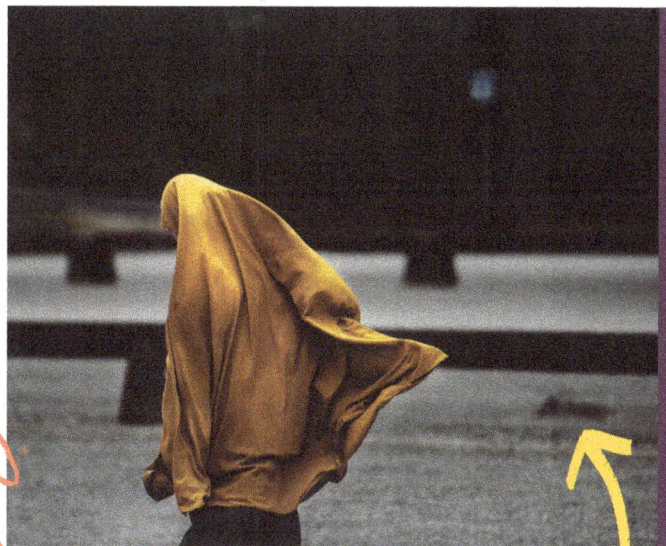

In Islamic culture it is considered very immodest for a woman to show her hair. Sometimes women must cover their entire face, leaving only their eyes revealed. It is only inside her own home with relatives that she is allowed to take her covering off.

In recent years devastating war has broken out across the Middle East. Many Syrian families are now living in refugee camps as they wait for a safe place to go.

CRAFT LIKE A
SYRIAN

In the Middle East there is an abundance of sand. Syrians use sand to make beautiful art. They carefully create intricate designs inside glass jars.

Various plants are used to dye sand different colors. These colors are layered inside the jars and a thin stick is used to create patterns in the layers. The designs are usually inspired by the scenery of the desert. The sand is made into the shape of camels walking across sand dunes, or palm trees near a pool of water.

Each jar is unique in size and shape, but a jar the size of the one in this picture contains about 20 million grains of sand! Imagine how many grains of sand cover a desert.

WANT TO GIVE IT A TRY?
Follow the steps on the next page to make your own sand art.

YOU'LL NEED:
- 1 glass jar
- craft sand (or salt)
- food coloring
- a funnel
- a long stick

PRAY ABOUT IT

As you create your sand art, take some time to pray for Syrians. Pray that they would hear about the God who created them and loves them.

1

Place a small amount of food coloring in your sand and mix it together until it is the desired shade. Make as many colors as you would like.

2

Placing the funnel on the top of the glass jar, layer your colored sand into the jar.

3

Continue in alternating layers.

4

If you would like to create your own patterns, try using a long stick to push sand down in various ways.

5

Fill your jar to the top and put the lid on it. You may glue it on to keep it in place, or just push it tightly.

6

Decorate with your new piece of art!

EVERYONE
NEEDS TO EAT

Why not try something new?

Chances are you've already tried this delicious Iranian dish, but have you ever made it yourself? It's easier than you might think. In Iraq hummus is usually eaten as one course in a large meal. If you're feeling ambitious, make a few other Middle Eastern recipes and have a feast with a friend or two. Make sure to tell them all that you have been learning about God's love for Muslims.

PRAY ABOUT IT

Thank God for all that you have learned and ask Him what He might want you to do with the new things you know.

THINK ABOUT IT

What is the most exciting thing you have learned?

Have you learned anything that has changed the way you think?

Hummus

ingredients

1 clove of garlic
1 can of chickpeas (drained)
1/3 cup of tahini (sesame paste)
3 tablespoons lemon juice
1/4 cup of water (or liquid from chickpea can)
1/4 cup of oil

directions

Step One:
Combine all ingredients in a food processor

Step Two:
Mix until smooth.

Step Three:
Transfer to a serving dish and serve with flatbread or veggies.

EAT LIKE
A SYRIAN

Many parts of Syria are dry and desert-like, but there is a region that sits between two rivers. This land is known as the "fertile crescent." Many fruits, vegetables, and grains are able to grow here. Most of the traditional Syrian meals are made with ingredients from this region.

Mealtime is usually a festive and casual time to enjoy friends and family. Guests are always served first and show their appreciation by over-eating. Typically meals begin with a "mezze" (appetizer) called kebabs. Then salad is served with a flatbread called khubaz. The main meal usually includes meat and vegetables.

One major staple in the Middle East is a dip made from garbanzo beans (some people also call them chickpeas). This dip is eaten with meat, rice, vegetables, and flatbread.

WANT TO GIVE IT A TRY? FOLLOW THE RECIPE ABOVE TO SEE IF YOU ENJOY EATING LIKE THE IRAQIS.

BUDDHIST

The last worldview we will look at is the *Buddhist* worldview. Let's learn about what Buddhist people believe.

WATCH THE VIDEO

Learn about what Buddhist people believe and how they live by watching this video: world-views.com/Buddhist

Unlike other religions, Buddhists do not believe in _____.
Eventually Siddhartha Gautama became known as _____ , which means _____ _____.
Buddhists believe that the cause of all suffering is our _____.
The end of suffering is called _____ and Buddhists believe it is accomplished through _____.

THINK ABOUT IT

Why do you think suffering happens?

Do you think it is important to live a selfless life? Why?

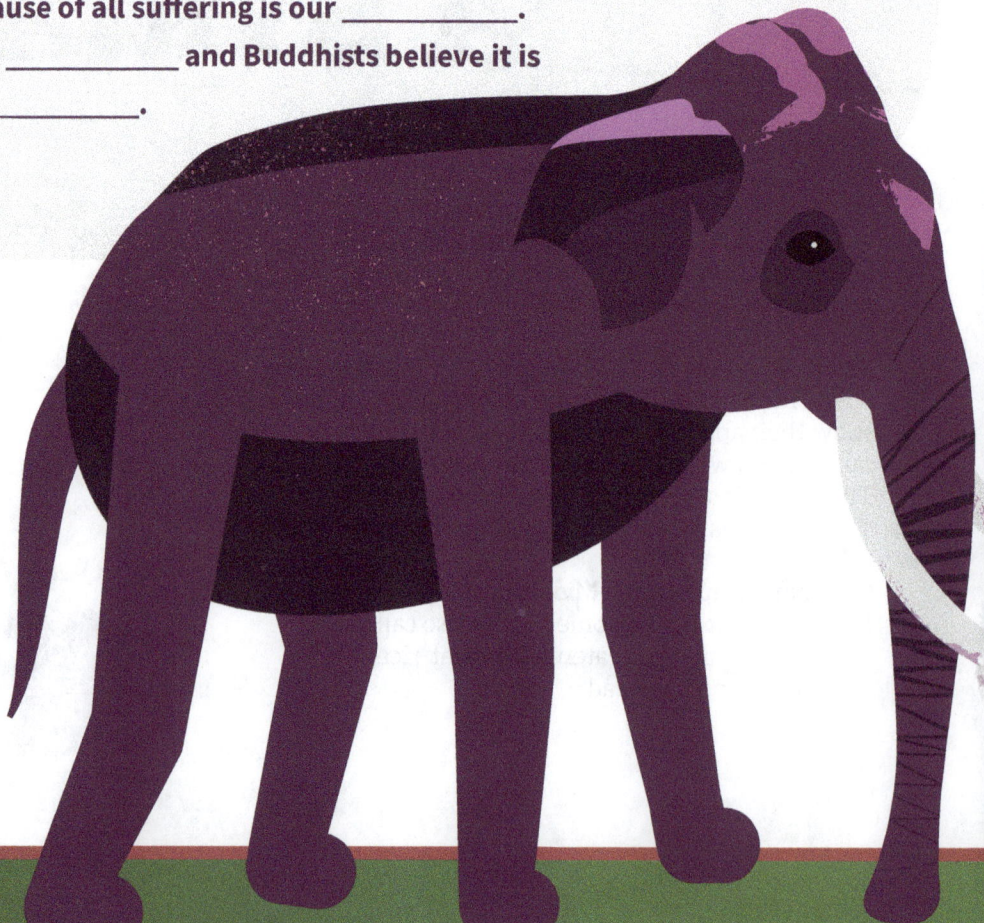

"ENLIGHTENMENT"

Buddhism isn't a set of clear rules; it's more like a set of teachings that are meant to point people in a direction. Everyone has to take his or her own journey towards self-enlightenment. The central teaching of Buddhism is known as the Eightfold Path:

RIGHT UNDERSTANDING

Buddhists believe there is a deeper reality than what we can easily see. To understand this reality, you must follow Buddhist teachings.

RIGHT INTENT

Once a person understands reality, he or she has to decide to live differently because of that knowledge. Right intent is the commitment to live in light of Buddhist teachings.

RIGHT SPEECH

Buddhists believe that it is important to avoid speech that is harmful such as lying, gossiping, and mean words.

RIGHT ACTION

To act the right way, a person must be considerate of others, make peaceful and honest choices, and keep away from drugs and alcohol.

RIGHT LIVELIHOOD

Buddhists believe that all life is equal in value and importance. A person should not have a job that disrespects any life, like weapon sales or butchery.

RIGHT EFFORT

In Buddhism, balance is important. A person shouldn't put too much effort or too little effort into self-enlightenment.

RIGHT MINDFULNESS

In Buddhism, people need to be aware of everything happening around them and inside of them like what they are feeling, thinking, and hearing, and seeing.

RIGHT CONCENTRATION

Buddhists believe that by meditating deeply, they can further their ability to see reality clearly and become more enlightened.

PRAY ABOUT IT

Spend some time today praying for Buddhist people. Pray that they would hear about a Savior who lived perfectly and pray that they would trust Him for their salvation.

HARVESTING
CROPS

LOOK UP MATTHEW 9:37-38 AND WRITE IT ON THE LINES BELOW:

_____

_____

_____

_____

Did you know that the world is like a field? Sharing the Gospel is like harvesting crops. Jesus says that there are plenty of people waiting to hear the Gospel, but there aren't very many people willing to tell them. There are many Buddhist people on the other side of the world who have never heard about Jesus. God is looking for laborers to send to them.

THINK ABOUT IT

What things keep people from becoming laborers in the harvest?
Is harvesting easy or hard work?

What does it mean that God is the Lord of the harvest?

BUDDH

WHERE IN THE WORLD ARE

IST PEOPLE?

CIRCLE THESE COUNTRIES ON THE MAP WHERE BUDDHIST PEOPLE CAN BE FOUND:

Myanmar   Cambodia   Thailand   Laos   Vietnam   Mongolia

DO CHRISTIANS AND BUDDHISTS HAVE THE SAME WORLDVIEW?

What does the Bible say about the way a Buddhist person views the world? Read through some Buddhist beliefs and then look up the corresponding Bible verses to see how they match up. After reading the verse write down what the Bible says and how that Buddhist belief compares.

ORIGINS

Buddhists do not believe the universe had a beginning. Our world is one of many that come and go in a never-ending cycle. The whole universe has always been and will never end.

HEBREWS 11:3 _____
_____
_____
_____

For a Buddhist, the beginning of life on earth isn't something we need to figure out. It shouldn't matter where we came from. But most Buddhists believe that we probably came from a process of natural evolution without the involvement of a creator.

PSALM 139:13-16 _____
_____
_____
_____

PSALM 121:1-2 _____
_____
_____
_____
_____

GOD

Buddhists do not believe in a god. But many believe in spiritual beings like angels, demons, demigods, spiritual monsters, and evil spirits.

PSALM 19:1-2 _____
_____
_____
_____

1 CORINTHIANS 8:6 _____
_____
_____
_____

Although many Buddhists do not believe that Buddha is a god, there are many traditions that worship him in various ways. Sometimes they pray to him or give offerings to his image.

LEVITICUS 26:1 _____
_____
_____
_____

MAN

Buddhist people believe we have a "black fire" burning within us, called "dawkha mee" which translates to "suffering fire." There are 10 "sins" that make up the fuel of this fire, but the main three are lawba, dawtha, and mawha which translate to greed, anger and ignorance. They believe that because of this fire, we get old, we get sick, and we die. Everyone is born with black fire, hence why we all suffer. It is our biggest problem.

PSALM 58:3

ROMANS 5:12

Buddhists believe that man's duty in life is to end suffering through enlightenment. If you can grow in knowledge and understanding, you will learn how to overcome selfish desires and end your suffering.

PROVERBS 3:5-6

PROVERBS 9:10-11

SIN

Buddhists believe they are sinning against the teachings of Buddha and the karma system. The Buddhist idea of the karma system is a magical justice force somewhere in the galaxy. It has no intelligent being behind it controlling it, however; it still affects every single person on this planet. If you make a good choice, you will be happy. These choices affect this life and they determine what you will be reincarnated as in the next life.

ROMANS 3:23

GALATIANS 6:8

Buddhists believe that we are always the cause of our suffering and we are always the solution to our suffering.

HEBREWS 12:6

2 CORINTHIANS 4:17

SALVATION

In Buddhism repentance is usually seen through offerings or acts of service (giving food to the poor or donating money to monks, etc.). They hope that through these repentances they will be able to cancel out bad merit/karma.

2 CORINTHIANS 5:10

_____
_____
_____
_____

Buddhists believe that the goal of life is to reach the point of ultimate enlightenment called nirvana. If a person has reached nirvana, he or she will not be reborn again, but will stop existing forever.

JAMES 1:12

_____
_____
_____
_____

HEBREWS 11:13-16

_____
_____
_____
_____

Buddha taught that everyone is responsible for achieving nirvana, and that everyone is capable of doing it without needing a god to save them. People are able to perfect their understanding, purify their minds, and develop infinite love and compassion on their own. Although Buddhists believe that it is possible, they live with a sense of hopelessness because they can't seem to reach nirvana even with their best efforts.

TITUS 2:11-12

_____
_____
_____
_____

DEATH

Buddhists believe that a person's soul leaves the body after death and goes on to one of six different realms. Where they go depends on their karma. If they were good, they are born into a realm like a temporary heaven. If they were bad, they are reborn into a realm like a temporary hell. There is also the realm where people are reborn on earth.

MATTHEW 25:31-46

_____
_____
_____
_____

Buddhists believe that there is no need to fear death if you have lived well. For the person who has good karma, death is an opportunity to move into a better position. It should be welcomed.

REVELATION 14:13

_____
_____
_____
_____

THINK ABOUT IT

Some Buddhist people care about similar things as Christians. How could God use that to help you connect with a Buddhist person?

Many Buddhist beliefs are very different from what the Bible says. How could you use those differences to share the Gospel?

SHARING
GOD'S STORY

How would you tell a Buddhist person about Jesus?

In many Buddhist cultures dance is a unique way to communicate important things. Spiritual stories, moral guidelines, and historical events are all depicted through special dances. If you are ever in a Buddhist culture, one way to communicate God's story may be through planning and performing a special dance.

One story they might find interesting is the story of creation. Growing up in a Buddhist culture means they probably haven't given much thought to where the world comes from. Or, if they have thought about it, they haven't found any answers within their culture's worldview. Buddha didn't believe it was important to know how the universe came into existence, but the Bible tells us how it all started.

Think about the story of creation found in Genesis. How could you depict this story through dance? If you meet a Buddhist, you might not want to start dancing right there on the sidewalk, but you can still talk to him or her about how it all began.

Plan three acts based on three main parts of the creation story. Write them down and then practice your performance.

ACT ONE

_____
_____
_____
_____
_____

ACT TWO

_____
_____
_____
_____
_____

ACT THREE

_____
_____
_____
_____
_____

PRAY ABOUT IT

Pray that Buddhists would hear about the God who created the world. Pray that they would desire to know Him.

BUDDHIST
BIBLE VERSE

Write down Pslam 37:4 on the lines below. For a Buddhist, desires are seen as a negative thing. They are the reason for suffering on earth and they are the reason it takes so long to reach nirvana. But we know that not all desires are bad, and God has given us desires that can lead us to Him.

Buddhist people need to know that God can satisfy the deep longings they feel because He put those longings inside their hearts. God wants Buddhists to experience the joys of knowing Him and to have the freedom to rejoice and delight in Him. Use this verse to remind you of the battle Buddhists face as they try to overcome their desires, and pray that they would learn about a God who can fulfill them.

_____

_____

_____

_____

_____

_____

_____

THINK ABOUT IT

Does the Bible teach that all desire is bad?

Why would it be important for a Buddhist person to understand right desire?

How do you think a Buddhist's ideas about desire might keep them from coming close to God?

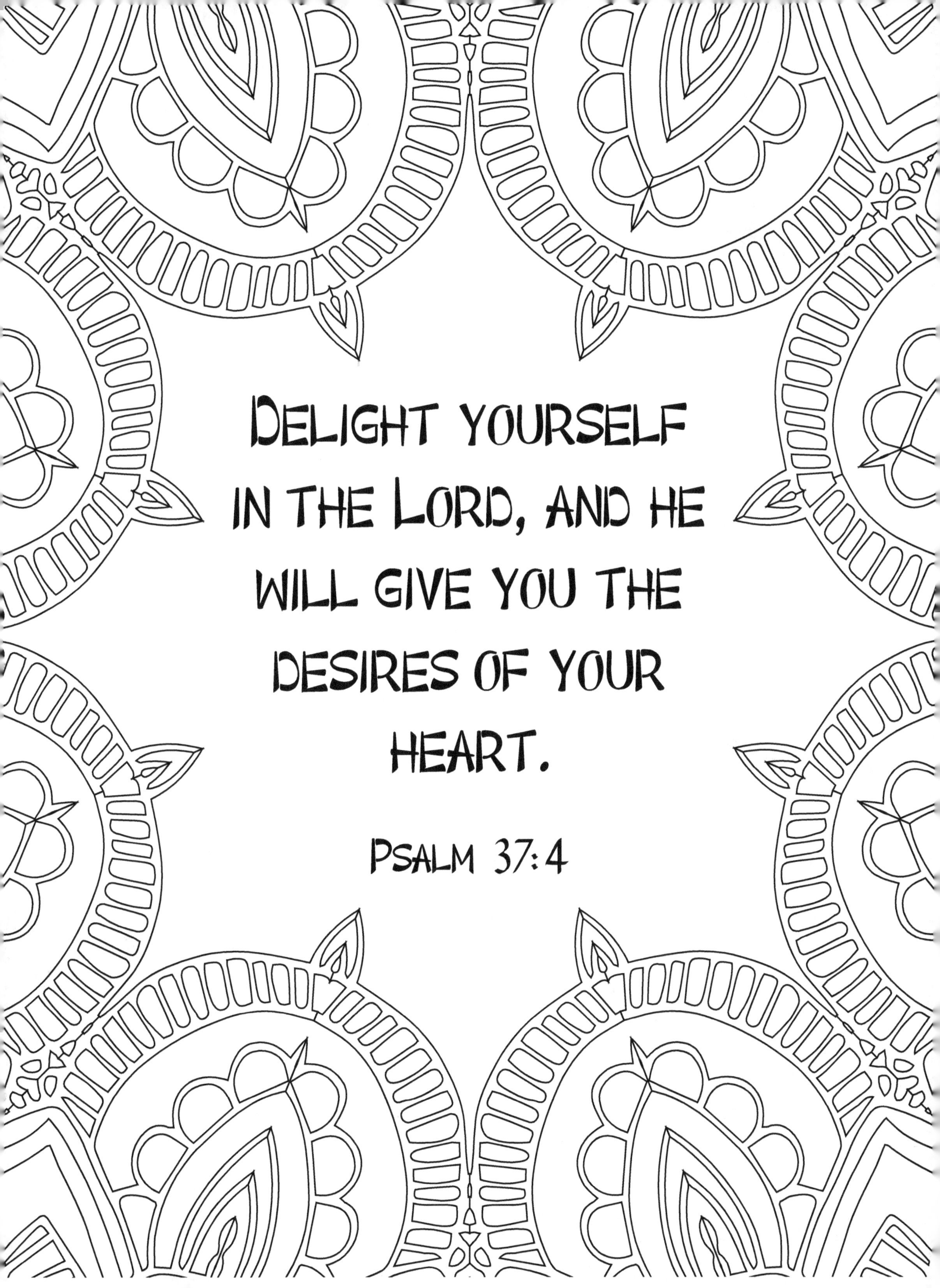

DELIGHT YOURSELF
IN THE LORD, AND HE
WILL GIVE YOU THE
DESIRES OF YOUR
HEART.

PSALM 37:4

THE
CULTURE

A person's worldview can be influenced by the culture he or she lives in. Read about the Burmese lifestyle and imagine what it would be like to live in their culture.

Myanmar is a country with many different landscapes. There are mountains, valleys, rivers, beaches, and even islands. Weather changes dramatically with each different region. The high mountains get snow and the low valleys get tropical monsoons.

Myanmar has many religious sights where temples and pagodas are built. The most famous pagoda is called the Shwedagon Pagoda. People believe that inside it are strands of hair from Buddha.

Myanmar is a very religious place. Some people are very Buddhist; others are very superstitious. Praying to Buddha and offering incense in worship are common occurrences.

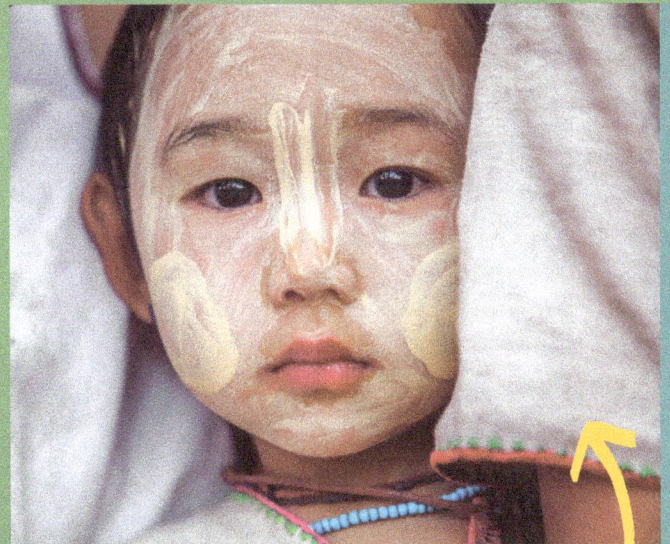

In Myanmar the sun can get really hot. Women paint their faces to protect their skin from the sun's rays and as a beauty treatment. This tradition is called thanakha. Sometimes it is applied in simple circles on the cheeks while other times it is painted on in elaborate designs.

Myanmar is home to many exotic animals. It has more tigers than almost anywhere in the world. Some animals are considered to mean good luck. If a person sees a white elephant in the wild, they believe they will have good fortune the rest of their lives.

PLAY LIKE THE
BURMESE PEOPLE

The traditional sport of Myanmar is called Chinlone. It has been a part of the culture for hundreds of years and started as a performance to entertain royalty.

The word Chinlone means "rounded basket." Chinlone balls are woven out of rattan and sound like a basket being kicked around.

Unlike other sports, Chinlone doesn't have winners or losers. The most important aspect of the game is to display beauty and good form as you interact with the ball and other players.

All players work together to keep a ball in the air. Forming a circle, players pass the ball to each other without letting it touch their hands or hit the ground. Watching this sport is almost like watching a dance as all six team members gracefully tap the ball to each other using their feet and knees.

WANT TO GIVE IT A TRY?
Follow the instructions to make your own Chinlone ball.

YOU'LL NEED:
- 12 paper clips
- 6 different color strips of paper about 12" long by 1/2" thick (it helps if you use the same colors as we did: pink, blue, orange, yellow, purple, and green)
- scissors
- tape

1

Tape the pink strip end to end to form a circle.
Set it aside.

2

Arrange the rest of the strips to match
the picture.

3

Put a paperclip at each joint to hold the
strips together.

4

Place the pink circle strip on top and weave the strips
through it: green over/purple under, yellow over/blue
under, orange over/green under, purple over/yellow
under, blue over/orange under.

5

Weave the strips on top of the ball using paper clips
to hold them together: orange over/green under,
purple over/yellow under, blue over/orange under,
green over/purple under, yellow over/blue under.

6

Unclip the joints below the pink strip.

7

Bring one end of the purple strip up to meet the other and tape it together to form a circle.

8

Weave the orange strip (joined to the blue strip) and bring it over the purple strip. Tape the orange ends together to form a circle.

9

Weave the blue strip under the purple strip. Tape the blue ends together to form a circle.

10

Weave the green strip over purple, under blue, and under orange. Tape the ends together to form a circle.

11

Weave the yellow strip over blue, under green, over orange, and under purple. Tape the yellow ends together to form a circle.

12

Remove paper clips and adjust the ball as needed. Try your hand at a game of Chinlone.

PRAY ABOUT IT

As you create your chinlone ball, take some time to pray for Burmese people. Pray that they would hear about the God who created them and loves them.

EVERYONE NEEDS TO EAT

Why not try something new?

No matter where you live or what you believe, there is a good chance you like dessert. But you probably haven't had a dessert quite like this before. Consider making this chilled coconut kyauk kyaw. Have a friend come over and help. You'll have to be patient because it needs to set in the fridge. While you wait you can tell your friend all that you have been learning about Buddhism and the Burmese.

PRAY ABOUT IT

Thank God for all that you have learned and ask Him what He might want you to do with the new things you know.

THINK ABOUT IT

What is the most exciting thing you have learned?

Have you learned anything that has changed the way you think?

Kyauk Kyaw

ingredients

2 1/2 cups water
2 teaspoons agar-agar powder
1/2 cup sugar
1 cup coconut milk
A pinch of salt

directions

Step One:
In a medium saucepan, stir together water, sugar, agar-agar, and salt.

Step Two:
Allow to boil on medium heat until the sugar and agar-agar dissolve completely.

Step Three:
Add coconut milk and boil for one minute.

Step Four:
Turn down the heat and simmer for two more minutes until you can see coconut solids separated on a spoon.

Step Five:
Pour into a pan and allow to set fully at room temperature.

Step Six:
Once set, place in refrigerator for several hours to cool. Serve chilled.

EAT LIKE THE
PEOPLE OF MYANMAR

In Myanmar, people don't eat as much dessert as we do here in America. When they do eat dessert, it is usually made with tropical fruits that are easy to find. One of their favorite desserts is called Kyauk Kyaw. It is a bit like coconut jello.

Coconut tress grow in many places in the region. Coconuts take almost a year before they are ready to be picked. They grow on tall trees that make them difficult to harvest. Many people use makeshift ladders attached to the tree, or a tall pruner pole to reach the fruit.

WANT TO GIVE IT A TRY? FOLLOW THE RECIPE ABOVE TO SEE IF YOU ENJOY EATING LIKE THE BURMESE.

THE REST OF
GOD'S STORY

SO CHRIST, HAVING BEEN OFFERED ONCE TO BEAR THE SINS OF MANY, WILL APPEAR A SECOND TIME, NOT TO DEAL WITH SIN BUT TO SAVE THOSE WHO ARE EAGERLY WAITING FOR HIM. HEBREWS 9:28

Did you know that Jesus is coming back? He's coming to earth again and when He does, it is going to be big! Everyone in the whole world will know about it. You see, Jesus won the battle with Satan a long time ago when He rose from the dead, but He hasn't announced His victory yet. When He returns, there will be no mistaking who He is: He is the Champion. He is the Rescuer. He is Lord.

And when He comes, He will make a new Heaven and a new Earth without Satan. Without **fear** or **weariness**. Where **no one can separate us from His love** and where **all our desires are fulfilled in Him**. It will be so amazing we **can't even begin to imagine it**. It's hard to wait for that, isn't it? But while we wait, there are some people who might be interested in this story. Some who haven't heard it, or don't understand it, or might not believe it. What a very important job we have to tell them about Jesus!

THINK ABOUT IT

Are you eagerly waiting for Jesus?

When Jesus comes back, you might get to meet the Tribal, Hindu, Unreligious, Muslim, and Buddhist people you have spent the last forty days praying for.

What will that be like?

Who do you know that has never heard this story?

Oh give thanks to the Lord; call upon his name;
make known his deeds among the peoples!
Sing to him, sing praises to him;
tell of all his wondrous works!
Glory in his holy name;
let the hearts of those who seek the Lord rejoice!
Sing to the Lord, all the earth!
Tell of his salvation from day to day.
Declare his glory among the nations,
his marvelous works among all the peoples!
Let the heavens be glad, and let the earth rejoice,
and let them say among the nations, "The Lord reigns!"
Let the sea roar, and all that fills it;
let the field exult, and everything in it!
Oh give thanks to the Lord, for he is good;
for his steadfast love endures forever!
"Save us, O God of our salvation,
and gather and deliver us from among the nations,
that we may give thanks to your holy name
and glory in your praise.
Blessed be the Lord, the God of Israel,
from everlasting to everlasting!"

CIRCLE THE WORDS FROM 1 CHRONICLES THAT SHOW ALL NATIONS WORSHIPING GOD. WHEN JESUS RETURNS, WE WILL BE PRAISING HIM WITH PEOPLE FROM EVERY LANGUAGE, COUNTRY, AND WORLDVIEW.